T0381021

THE GRASS FLUTE ZEN MASTER

Opposite: Yokoyama playing the grass flute at Kaikoen Park

The Grass Flute Zen Master: Sodo Yokoyama

Arthur Braverman

COUNTERPOINT • CALIFORNIA

Library of Congress Cataloging-in-Publication Data
is available.

Cover and Interior design by Gopa & Ted2, Inc.

ISBN 978-1-61902-913-2

COUNTERPOINT
Los Angeles and San Francisco, CA
www.counterpointpress.com

150773343

For Ari, Oliver and Sanae:
The next generation

Contents

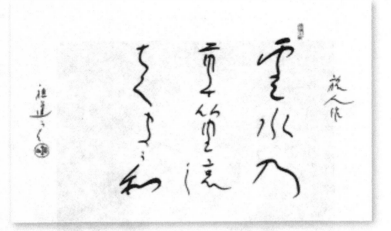

unsui no
kusabue kanashi
chikuma gawa

Floating cloud monk
Plays leaf whistle soulfully
Chikuma River

—Written by a traveler
(from *Living and Dying in Zazen*)

Sodo Yokoyama practicing zazen

1

In Search of a Japanese Maharshi

I step outside of the Komoro Train Station into the after-
noon sun—an unusually dry sunny day for early June in central Japan. The year is 2014. The station is approximately
fifty yards from the entrance to Kaikoen Park, where Sodo
Yokoyama spent more than twenty years meditating, playing the leaf flute, and brushing beautiful calligraphy.

I've come here to meet Joko Shibata, Yokoyama's sole disciple. Joko and I have become friends since my first interview with him in 1996. I try to visit him whenever I come to
Japan. Our connection, of course, is Joko's late teacher, the
hermit of Kaikoen Park, Sodo-san, as he is familiarly called.
I'm trying to learn more about this colorful Zen man who
spent the last twenty-two years of his life demonstrating to
Japanese who happen to be strolling through the park what
it means to be forever young.

As I sit on a rickety wooden bench outside the station
waiting for Joko, I reflect on my first encounter with the
Grass Flute Zen Master. It was autumn 1970. Together with

two friends from Antaiji Temple, Steve and Lew, I came to meet this unique Zen man I'd so often heard about. At the time my knowledge of Sodo-san was a mixture of fact and myth.

"There's a monk named Sodo-san, a brother disciple of Uchiyama's, who lives in the woods in Nagano Prefecture. He spends his days sitting in zazen, brushing poems, and playing music on a leaf," Lew said.

The image appealed to both of us. Lew and I had read the life of Ramana Maharshi, the early twentieth-century Indian saint, who left his home at seventeen years old to live on a sacred mountain in Southern India. Ramana stayed in a cave on Arunachala Mountain, in deep *samadhi*, content to just *be*. Some people who lived at the foot of the mountain recognized that the boy, Ramana, was spiritually advanced and took it upon themselves to take care of him. Had they not been there he would surely have starved to death.

I'd come to Japan secretly hoping to meet a Japanese *Maharshi*. I hoped Sodo-san was my man.

When we arrived at the park at 8:30 that morning we were told that the Grass Flute monk wouldn't arrive before 10. I knew by then that Sodo-san didn't live in the woods; that he spent his nights in a boardinghouse and his days in the park. Still I assumed he would be in the park by five or six in the morning. The mythic aspect of my image of this monk started to crumble.

We left the park and went to the nearest grocery store and picked up some fruit and tea as an offering. When we returned a little after 10, he was sitting, legs folded, his bottom resting on his ankles in formal Japanese *seiza* position, his torso long and upright, giving the false impression that he was a tall man. He wore monks' work clothes and a black beret, and his dress and carriage were dignified, suggesting to me a traditional upbringing. He was a thin man with narrow classical features.

Seeing three foreigners standing near him, he picked up a leaf from a bowl of leaves in water, placed it on his lower lip, and holding it in place with two fingers of his right hand played "Old Folks at Home." It was the funkiest version of the Stephen Foster tune I'd ever heard.

Sodo Yokoyama practicing zazen near Antaiji Temple. Though a shy man by nature, he practiced zazen wherever he was. Here he is in the fields around Antaiji Temple, meditating under the open sky.

2

Noodles and Memories of a Leaf-Blowing Monk

It was a few minutes before noon when I'd arrived at the Komoro Train Station and I didn't want to disturb Joko when he was about to have lunch. I knew he would invite me to join him and run around to prepare something more substantial than the meager fare he usually made for himself. That's the way Japanese are. So, before calling him, I went to a noodle shop on the second floor above a pharmacy across from the station to have some lunch.

The place was small. Five tables and a counter. Though it was noon there were no other customers. I sat at the counter. A small thin woman I'd guessed to be in her early fifties, grey streaks in her permed black hair, tied in the back, came to take my order. I assumed she was the owner. The TV was on, an NHK serial drama that I'd been watching at my in-laws' home in Sakai City, and I immediately became absorbed in it.

"What will you have, sir?"

I ordered *udon* noodle soup with *tororo* (grated yam).

The story on the TV dramatized the life of Hanako Muraoka, the woman who translated *Anne of Green Gables* into Japanese. She grew up during the Taisho period, just before the fascists' takeover of the country. This period from 1911 to 1925 is referred to as the Taisho Democracy, a brief interlude in the history of Japan, when the influence of the democratic ideals of the West seeped into the consciousness of Japanese intellectuals.

Though Hanako Muraoka was born at the end of the Meiji era, her coming of age was during that Taisho period when individual expression was no longer frowned upon by many of the young learned people. If Sodo-san was reading some of the popular writers of this period, since he, too, came of age at this time, he may very well have been influenced by the same democratic spirit of the times.

"Your *udon*," the woman said, as she placed a tray with a bowl of noodles and a small dish of daikon pickles in front of me.

I thanked her, split my chopsticks and started eating while I kept my eyes and ears on the drama of this young, educated Hanako returning to her country village.

Hanako's father had sent her to a Christian school in Tokyo over the objections of the rest of her family, when he recognized her special love of books.

The matron was watching the drama from the open door between the dining room and the kitchen. She seemed to be mustering up courage to start a conversation with me.

"You like Japanese drama?"

Hanako Muraoka

"Yes, and I have a particular interest in the life of Hanako Muraoka."

"Really," she said, followed by silence. She appeared surprised and didn't know what to say next.

"Hanako grew up during the same time as the Grass Flute monk who used to play the leaf in the park across the way," I said, hoping to put things in context. But it seemed to confuse her even more.

She began to wipe the counter. Then a lightbulb appeared to go off in her head, "Oh, you mean the NHK monk. I never saw him, but my husband told me about him. You see I'm from Saku, but my husband grew up in Komoro. When he was a kid, he and his friends would go to listen to the monk play music and enjoy his company. They all picked leaves from the trees and tried to imitate the monk, but eventually gave up. They loved to joke with him. 'He was just like a kid, like one of us,' my husband said."

Once an NHK TV crew came to the park to film an interview with Sodo-san by a nun named Aoyama. From that time on, people from Komoro figured Sodo-san must be an important person if a major national TV station came all that way to film an interview and tell his story.

In an article Uchiyama wrote for the magazine *Tsukumo* about visiting Sodo-san, his older brother in the Dharma, he referred to Sodo-san as the Pied Piper of Hamelin, because when he lived at Antaiji in Kyoto groups of children often followed him around. Uchiyama wrote of the TV program about Sodo-san, "I'm sure many viewers seeing him on television, sitting in the park with the Japan Alps in the background, recognized the leaf-playing monk they knew from childhood."

I've met many monks and a few Zen Masters since coming to Japan in 1969, and none of them manifest an individual sensibility to the degree that Sodo-san did. He was truly an example of someone who expressed the ideals of many of the writers of the Taisho democracy—a faith in the value of individualism. This was a radical departure from the Japanese ideal that dominated the culture both before and after those fifteen years—a belief in absolute purity and selflessness.

In Sodo-san's writing there is very little about his childhood, just a page or two out of three hundred in his journal and very little in recordings of his conversations. Neither Joko, his lone disciple, nor Sodo-san's nephew, whom I visited five years ago, shed any light on his early experiences.

According to the editor of his journals, after Sodo-san met his teacher Kodo Sawaki, he burned most of his previous journal entries. So, with the few remaining notes of his childhood experiences from his journals and things he said when I visited him in the park, and my knowledge of the culture he grew up in, I hope to give a picture of how Sodo-san became the person he did.

I finished my meal watching the installment of Hanako and *Anne*. I thanked the lady and complimented her on her cooking.

She bowed to me and said, "Yes, the NHK monk. Wait until I tell my husband when he gets home. He'll be thrilled. The NHK monk," she repeated and bowed once more, adding, "Please come again."

3

Sitting with Joko by the Bamboo Grove

So here I am now, a box of sweet cakes I just picked up from a souvenir shop next to the station, waiting for Joko to meet me as he instructed. I always enjoy my time with Joko. He is lively and there is no posturing about him. From our first meeting, he appeared so open I felt none of the tightness I usually feel when meeting a Japanese monk. Physically, too, he looks very ordinary. I want to say like the average Japanese man you might meet on the street, but that wouldn't help give you a picture of him. He is average height, medium build, wears thick horn-rimmed glasses that seem to barely stay on his flat nose and has an overbite that would make leaf-blowing, if he were so inclined to imitate his teacher, difficult. He is neither musical nor accomplished as a calligrapher. But he has something that makes him special, to this story at least: a complete devotion to the teaching of Sodo Yokoyama.

    I don't want to give the impression that Joko and I see

eye to eye on all matters, Buddhist or otherwise. We have disagreed over the years on some major interpretations of some words handed down by teachers in and outside of his lineage. The fact that we can debate these issues I attribute to a real friendship.

Joko has lived by himself since the death of his teacher thirty-four years ago. His daily life consists of zazen, attending a small vegetable garden, and studying the writings of Sodo-san, Kodo Sawaki, and Dogen Zenji. He has little contact with the outside world. A few monks, laymen, and one foreigner besides me have dropped by his house (which he refers to as the *Kokazan Senri* Temple). The name was taken from a phrase Sodo-san often brushed: *ko ka* is the fragrant mist of incense; and *sen ri* is a thousand *ri* or four thousand kilometers. The fragrant mist of incense, I imagine, stands for the Dharma and a thousand *ri* means "everywhere."

Joko has built a Zen meditation room that can seat ten to fifteen people, in order to spread his teacher's Dharma, but the room lies empty most of the time. Even when Joko sits in zazen, which he does for a good part of his day, he usually sits in an enclosed porch facing Mount Asama, a live volcano, rather than in his meditation room.

Joko's understanding of the intricacies of zazen practice is profound. Like his teacher, he has devoted his life to the practice, and can talk about it as long as one is willing to listen. When I think of Joko's practice, I think of the seventh ox-herding picture, "Ox Forgotten, the Man Left Alone." He hasn't gone out into the world, as did his teacher.

There is no better expression of the tenth ox-herding picture, "Entering the Market Place With Giving Hands," than Sodo-san sitting in the bamboo grove off the main path in Kaikoen Park, playing the leaf, sitting in zazen, and selling his brushed musical compositions.

My musings are interrupted by the sound of a motor scooter pulling up alongside me. Joko in his black monk's work clothes and motorcycle helmet gets off the bike, removes his helmet, puts the scooter up on its stand, and bows to me.

"Arthur, thanks for coming all this way to visit me," he says and sits next to me.

I bow in return and tell him how good it is to see him again. Two and a half years have gone by since my last visit.

Joko stands up, walks over to a signboard by the bus stop, studies it, and returns to the bench. "The bus doesn't leave for another hour and a half so we have some time. Shall we go to my teacher's monument? It's a beautiful sunny day."

Taking guests to pay homage at the monument to Sodo-san is Joko's duty and pleasure.

We enter Kaikoen Park and walk about a quarter of a mile to the bamboo grove where Sodo-san spent over twenty years in his Temple Under the Sky. We sit on a bench across from a box on a stand with a photo of Sodo-san smiling and a bunch of children sitting around him. To the left is a rock with a poem carved in it in Sodo-san's calligraphy:

Floating cloud monk
Plays leaf whistle soulfully
Chikuma River.

We sit there for about ten minutes, saying nothing.

By the monument
under the pine tree
he plays the leaf flute
I Iisten joyfully
the pleasures of travel.

—A traveler's poem

4

The Magic Box with the Sound of the Universe

I stare at the box and the rock slab with Sodo-san's calligraphy carved on it, and a rush of memories flood my brain.
The first time I saw that box I had no idea what it was about.
I had taken my daughter to see the Japanese countryside in
2003. Up to that time, though she'd often been to Japan, all
she'd ever seen were the big Japanese cities, Osaka, Tokyo,
and the home of her grandparents, Sakai. She wanted to see
the countryside and I wanted to visit Joko Shibata. I decided
to do both together. I didn't know how she would feel about
spending time with a monk who would surely talk our ears
off about Sodo-san and zazen. I worried myself for no reason. Joko was his gracious self, making her feel at home,
taking us to see some of the scenic country around Komoro.

We had time then before Joko would come to meet us at
the station, so I took Nao to the park looking for the spot
where Sodo-san used to set up his Temple Under the Sky.
The rock slab with his calligraphy marked the spot, but what
was that box? I was feeling choked up—having found the

spot and remembering having met Sodo-san thirty-some-odd years before, and now, thirty-one years later, showing my daughter a part of my world that existed before she was born.

I noticed a button on the box and pressed it with my finger. At that point I thought I knew what was coming. Still, when the funky sound of the leaf whistle rendering a tune, not in perfect pitch in accordance with a music aficionado, but as soulful as any of the old blues masters, I had to hold back tears.

"I finally understand zazen," Joko says, waking me from my reverie.

I have the feeling I've heard this from him before. Maybe he sees something more deeply each time we meet, and it feels like discovering zazen for the first time. I want to question him about it, when a group of tourists comes by and reads the calligraphy carved on the rock slab. They appear to be a family, three generations. The old man, hair grey and thinning, reads the haiku on the rock slab and explains the meaning to the man I assume to be his son or son-in-law. The young man listens with interest or politeness while the three children, grandchildren I guess, look bored. The young woman is pointing out a flower to her mother or mother-in-law; both women appear equally uninterested in the old man's explanation of the haiku. The old man walks over to the box and pushes the button. They listen to the recording of Sodo-san playing the leaf, which even catches the attention of the kids.

The funky music is unmistakable, but the words I can't get.

"Is that one of Sodo-san's compositions?" I ask Joko.

"No, it's Toson Shimazaki's poem put to music, 'Song of a Traveler's Weary Heart by Chikuma River.'"

I know that Toson was a famous Japanese writer, and that his poem is about the ruins that are now Kaikoen Park. I will have to learn more about him as part of my investigation into the mind of Sodo-san.

"How much of an influence did Toson have in Sodo-san's decision to settle down here?" I ask Joko.

"How much of an influence . . ." Joko repeats my words, cocking his head.

I am surprised once again at how little this teacher and disciple appear to have discussed other than Buddhism and meditation. Sodo-san must not have talked about his past to Joko, who may have felt it rude to pry. It puzzles me, however, how you can live together for so long and not pry a little. Not to say how much more difficult my work will be trying to learn what brought Sodo-san to choose to live his unique lifestyle.

"I wonder what kind of leaves he used to make such beautiful music?" the old man says out loud, but to no one in particular.

"*Masaki* leaf," Joko says, getting the attention of the whole family at once. He seems happy to move to a subject about which he feels confident.

Masaki leaf? Another word to look up later.

"Only *masaki*?" the old man asks.

"Only *masaki*," Joko says with confidence.

The kids are ready to move on, so the old man bows to Joko and follows the family to the next place on their schedule. Maybe they will go to the monument to Toson, or to the inn where the poet used to go for the hot springs.

I imagine it is only people as old as the grandfather who are interested in Sodo-san and Toson, the kids wanting something more exciting, and the father and mother hoping to please both their children and their parents at one time. Given the different interests of the children and grandparents, they have quite a balancing act. When their duties in keeping the family happy are over, I imagine the young man will be looking forward to a game of golf or relaxing with a beer watching a ballgame on TV.

"We'd better start walking back," Joko says, looking at his watch.

We stand, bow to the monument to Sodo-san, and follow the path to the exit from the park. A little way along the path, Joko turns and walks over to some shrubs a little taller than him and picks a leaf from them. He brings it over and hands it to me.

"*Masaki no ha*," he says. It's an oval leaf about two inches long with finely serrated margins.

I hold the leaf with my fingers, place it between my lips, and fail miserably at making anything other than the sound of wind. Joko chuckles at each of my failed attempts, as we continue walking out of the park.

Sodo-san playing the leaf in the park

Song of a Traveler's Weary Heart
by Chikuma River

Near old Komoro Castle
White clouds and the sadness of an uprooted traveler
No green chickweed sprouting
No young grasses for a suitable carpet
Silver white blankets the hill
Light snow floes melting under the sun
Though warm in the light
No fragrance throughout the fields
Just a faint spring mist
A few patches of green barely
A group of travelers
Hurry across the road between fields
Asama no more visible in the coming darkness
The grass flute Saku's sad song
Chikuma River waves on the sixteenth moon day
I climb to the hut near the shore
Drink cloudy sake as it is
Pass the night amusing myself.

Toson Shimazaki

5

Fragrant Mist Travels a Thousand Leagues

I take the bus to Joko's home/temple. He's named it *kokazan senriji.*

Kokasenri was brushed often by Sodo-san, meaning "fragrant mist travels a thousand leagues." Temples in Japan have mountain names and temple names: *san* means "mountain" and *ji* means "temple." So *kokazan senriji* means "Fragrant Mist Mountain, A Thousand League Temple."

Joko rides his motorbike and meets me at the entrance. His house looks like anything but a temple. Even for a Japanese private home, it is particularly nondescript. It exemplifies its owner's need for utility and lack of interest in anything ostentatious. It is almost at the top of an uphill road with a village graveyard just below and a factory dormitory above where the road ends. Joko cultivates a small vegetable garden, which gets larger each time I visit. He used to sit ten hours a day, but perhaps his knees and back can no longer sustain such a severe practice, hence more time for the vegetables.

We enter the vestibule, take off our shoes, step up to the hallway and wash our hands in the kitchen on our right. Then we go to the meditation hall that Joko has built in memory of his teacher.

"My teacher had planned to build a place where people could practice zazen, but he never got the chance, so I did it in his stead," Joko once told me.

I light an incense stick in front of the altar where two photos, one of Sodo-san and the other of Kodo Sawaki, are placed, and we bow to the two masters. Then we backtrack to the adjoining tatami dining area. I sit on a mat at a low table and Joko brings us tea and some sweets. We don't waste time on small talk, but get right into subjects about Sodo-san that I've been contemplating throughout the year.

"I'd like to talk about your teacher's unusual practice of playing his musical compositions on a leaf. His practice of zazen of course is central to his life, but a man of zazen will not be as unique to readers because there are many. Playing his own musical compositions on a leaf for passing travelers makes him one of a kind as far as I know." I hope this doesn't disappoint Joko, for whom zazen is the centerpiece of his life.

"Yes, my teacher was an artist as well as a man of Zen. I'm glad you understand that. Together with a fellow who understands music and how to transform my teacher's tunes into computer-generated music, we are producing a CD of his music, electronically."

No, no, no, I want to say, but I don't. You can't produce that funky sound with electronic music. I've even heard a chorus sing Sodo-san's songs beautifully, but sounding like Pavarotti singing Robert Johnson's "Sweet Home Chicago." Beautiful, maybe; funky, no way.

"Did the fact that Toson Shimazaki lived in Komoro and wrote the poem with reference to the sad song played on a leaf influence Sodo-san's decision to move to Kaikoen Park?" I ask, wanting to move away from electronic music.

"I don't know. He certainly had a chance to learn of Toson's poems. Toson was a famous poet when Roshi was in school during the Taisho period. He read the classics at the time, I'm sure. But whether he read Toson back then I really don't know."

I'm once again surprised at how Joko could live with his teacher for so many years and not know anything about his pre-zazen life. I realize Japanese rarely talk about themselves unless they are specifically questioned, with the exception of zazen in Sodo-san's case. He'd certainly felt obligated to talk with Joko about zazen and Buddhism. After all, it was Buddhism and zazen, Yokoyama's zazen, that propelled Joko to 'push' his way into his teacher's life.

Toson was a renowned poet, an innovator of a new Japanese poetry, a result of his studies of the romantic poets of Europe. He also wrote confessional novels, called "I

Novels," one exposing an affair he had with his older brother's daughter, which drew strong criticism from the literary world.

He was born in Gifu Prefecture and moved with his family to the Kiso Mountains in Nagano Prefecture. He was among a group of writers who were born in the provinces and educated in private universities in Tokyo.

Educated in the Japanese classics as well as the modern writers and philosophers from the West, Toson seems to have been drawn to confessional writing as a form of cleansing for past sins. After studying at university in Tokyo, he went to live in France for three years.

In Sodo-san's journals, the ones he didn't destroy, there is no mention of Toson, but he often recited and played a tune to Toson's poem, "Song of a Traveler's Weary Heart by Chikuma River." There is a pathos in Toson's poetry that I sense in many of Sodo-san's poems. For example:

> (On the death of his brother in the battle off Midway Island, June 5, 1942)
> *When I look at Neptune's blue sea,*
> *I see my brother,*
> *I want to pray to the sea.*

(In October of the same year, his mother died)
A field far from home
Thoughts of mother
Gone forever
Fill me with grief.

The following poem reminds me of Toson's "Song of a Traveler's Weary Heart by Chikuma River" (above) with its feeling of despair at a world one cannot control:

Begging along the avenue
A truck splashes sludge in its track
Mud spatters on my sleeves.

I want to understand this dark side of Sodo-san, which appears to contrast so pointedly with the man I remember and with the many photos of his cheerful face in the park.

Sodo-san serving tea at Kaikoen Park

6

A Pheasant Teaches Sodo-san about Zazen

It's evening and Joko and I sit a period of zazen before calling it a night. A good part of the day was spent listening to Joko's exposition on zazen. He never tires of talking about zazen, and though I have much more about Sodo-san on my mind than zazen, I enjoy listening to Joko's animated praise of the practice. He quoted from Kodo Sawaki more often than from his own teacher, and it makes me think of Sawaki, the controversial Zen master known by the epithet "Homeless Kodo."

Sawaki, who traveled the country teaching monks and laypeople and never stayed for any length of time in one place, was admired for a lifestyle reminiscent of the old Zen eccentrics. He said he was the most deluded person in the world, and that he practiced zazen because only then did he experience the world of the Buddha. It was that attitude, I believe, that caught the attention of the young Sodo-san at a time when he was feeling confused about what to do with his life.

Sodo-san was a fan of baseball as a child and often used baseball terms to describe very 'un-baseball-like' activities. He described zazen as the only thing in his life that felt 'safe.' His use of the word 'safe' was clearly the baseball meaning. All other things in life, he added, were 'over run,' the Japanese word for getting caught off the base. Though Sodo-san had his own unique way of describing zazen, the influence of his teacher is unmistakable.

Sawaki was quoted as saying, "I might have been a gangster, a yakuza boss, or even a murderer had I not come across the teachings of the Buddha." The teachings of the Buddha for Sawaki meant zazen. He also said, "All of Buddhism is a footnote to zazen."

I can't think of two people more different in temperament than Kodo Sawaki and Sodo Yokoyama. The former raised in the slums of Tsu City—the stepson of a gambler and his eleventh wife, a former prostitute—a boy wild by nature. The latter born into the family of retainers for the Toyama clan, the youngest of three brothers, who seems to have been given special consideration by a father who was otherwise quite stern. Perhaps his father recognized the gentleness in his youngest son and worried about his future survival in a world in great flux as a result of the Meiji revolution. But both men followed their own drummers, and I imagine Sawaki recognized his young disciple's uniqueness and perhaps was envious of his gentility. I also imagine that Sawaki, like Sodo-san's father, felt a need to protect his new, young delicate disciple.

Kodo Sawaki had no temple when his new disciple shaved his head, so he sent Sodo-san to a temple run by Eiko Hashimoto, a Zen master for whom Sawaki had great respect. Hashimoto was on a list of teachers Shunryu Suzuki gave to his first American disciple, Grahame Petchey, when Grahame was sent to Japan. Along with Sawaki, Hashimoto was someone who Suzuki felt could answer questions Grahame had about Zen that Suzuki, himself, felt unable to answer.

Though the situation when Sawaki sent his new disciple off to a temple of a Zen man he highly respected was different from when Sodo-san sent Joko to Eiheiji Temple for three years, there were some interesting parallels. Sawaki had experienced the constrictions of monastic life once he had learned the basics and knew he had to move on to what he felt was his road to understanding more deeply the meaning of Zen. Staying in one place training monks was something he relegated to students of his, while he lived the life of an itinerant monk. The old masters he respected were the eccentrics like the beggar Unkei Tosui who, after years of Zen study, refused to be tied down to a temple and spent his life in towns and cities, a loner who valued his freedom above all.

Though Sodo-san did settle down in one place after having trained for many years in temples and monasteries, he did so on his own terms in the spirit of another Zen eccentric, Taigu Ryokan, who was often compared to the beggar Tosui. Taigu Ryokan was known to the people of Japan as the lovable Ryokan-san. Ryokan-san, a poet and calligrapher, refused to take charge of a temple, preferring to live alone. He composed beautiful poems and brushed delicate calligraphy, both recognized as some of the best works of art of eighteenth- and nineteenth-century Japan. I don't know how much Sawaki perceived of the free spirit in his new disciple, but I will guess that he recognized something of Sodo-san's need to follow his own path, as Sawaki had done in his younger years. I believe Sawaki felt that his friend Hashimoto would not quell that need in Sodo-san.

"Sawaki Roshi understood my teacher's need to express himself with his poetry," Joko tells me over tea the next morning, "when he suggested Sodo-san go to Kyushu where he would meet Kumamoto no Okina."

This, of course, was after Sodo-san had spent some time studying with Eiko Hashimoto. Kumamoto no Okina was the nickname for Shuseki Saito, a medical doctor, poet, and calligrapher. He was a follower of Sawaki and when Sodo-san went to Kumamoto Prefecture to live alone and continue his practice for a period of four and a half years, Okina befriended the young disciple of his teacher. Until Okina's death in 1973, Sodo-san had a regular correspondence with him, discussing poetry and their understanding of Buddhism and zazen. Okina seems to have had a great influence on Sodo-san's approach to Zen.

One of Sodo-san's epiphanies was when he sat in zazen in the mountains and a pheasant seemed to join him. He later turned it into a *waka* poem:

Years ago
meditating in the mountains
a pheasant appeared
and stared
at my zazen.

He sent the poem to Okina, who commented that animals feel unthreatened when one's attention is not on them. For Sodo-san the pheasant incident had an even deeper meaning than that of his mentor's interpretation. Yes, the pheasant felt unthreatened by the zazen posture, but not because the attention was not on the bird. He believed that the zazen posture was an expression of a Universal consciousness, and hence unthreatening to the pheasant.

Sodo Yokoyama and his teacher Kodo Sawaki

7

Always a Little Out of Tune

Joko published a book of his teacher's writing seven years ago titled *The Universal Seated Form of the Buddha*, (普勧坐相みほとけ or *fukan zasou mihotoke* in Japanese). As the title states, the book contains Sodo-san's writing on Zen meditation or zazen. A major section of the book covers Sodo-san's writing about his teacher, Kodo Sawaki, and Sawaki's views on zazen. It is not surprising that Joko should concentrate on his teacher's view of zazen since that's what attracted him to Sodo-san and sustains him to this day.

One small part of the book, which for me is especially valuable, is a selection of Sodo-san's songs with a CD to accompany them. You can see a side of Sodo-san that Joko respects but has not tried to emulate. He sees his teacher as an artist but doesn't seem to feel that artistic drive in himself.

With the help of his friend and mentor, Kumamoto no Okina, and the instructions from Koumyo Shibutani, a musician he met in Kyoto, Sodo-san transformed his poems into beautiful musical compositions. Taking his poems, composing music for them, and then with his delicate calligraphy brushing sheets of music, Sodo-san was able to express his unique lifestyle; the life of a most colorful monk.

I suspect Sodo-san first played his compositions on the leaf for anyone interested, and when requests for his music grew and people offered to pay for his calligraphy, he got the idea of selling sheets of brushed musical compositions.

For me, Sodo-san's leaf-blowing music is a porthole into his past, one that he seems to have covered up when he burned his early diaries after meeting his teacher, Kodo Sawaki. He incorporated his talent for music, calligraphy, and poetry into his life as a Zen man (which officially began in his thirtieth year, when he met Sawaki). His artistic talent must have had an earlier beginning.

I am reminded of Walt Whitman, a favorite of Sodo-san's, who appears to have become a poet at thirty-seven years old with the first edition of *Leaves of Grass* but for whom that collection of poems was brewing inside him long before he wrote the book.

Sodo-san referred to his music as "always a little out of tune." For him that was the beauty of the leaf as an instrument. A literal translation of 'sandlot baseball' from Japanese to English would be 'grass baseball.' So Sodo-san would call his music 'sandlot music.'

Suzuki Roshi, the beloved transmitter of Soto Zen to America in the 1950s and '60s, lectured about four horses of different degrees from excellent to poor, and how the poor horse has the most difficulty learning. We misunderstand Zen when our goal is to become the best horse. The Buddha, Suzuki said, with his mercy cares most about the poor one. I see the same spirit displayed by Sodo-san. In his music and his zazen, he never saw himself as accomplished, but that was okay because the Buddha took care of him. What he may have lacked in talent, he had received through the Buddha in spirit.

The Buddha appeared to Sodo-san through his father, through Kodo Sawaki, Shuseki Saito, Koumyo Shibutani, and all the travelers who strolled through Kaikoen Park in Komoro. He appears to have come upon his unique lifestyle after training as a Zen monk at monasteries in Saku (next door to Komoro), Tokyo, Kumamoto, and Antaiji in Kyoto. But I suspect the seeds for the last twenty-two years of his life, sitting in a park meditating and playing music on the leaf for passing travelers, had been brewing in his heart long before.

From what I heard about his life at Antaiji, like most artists, he followed his heart. He may have attempted to live the life of a conventional monk, but he could only go so far before his true mind would show itself. Uchiyama, his brother disciple and caretaker of Antaiji, loved his friend, but was frustrated at how difficult it was to get Sodo-san to follow a prescribed monastic way.

Few monasteries in Japan attempt to translate the teachings of Zen master Dogen, the founder of Japanese Soto Zen, in its purest form as does Antaiji. Dogen's emphasis on zazen above all is the monastery's main focus. All other practices are truly subordinate to zazen. That was Kodo Sawaki's instruction, which Kosho Uchiyama followed when he took over after Sawaki's death.

The temple became a magnet for students, monks, and laypeople, who felt that zazen was the true way to an enlightened life. Sodo-san, too, believed zazen should be the center of his life, and though he left Antaiji to follow his calling, Antaiji never left him. Many of his poems and songs are about his life when he lived there, and the temple seems to have symbolized for him a house where the spirit of his late teacher, Sawaki, and the founder of Soto Zen, Dogen, still lives. But there was another authority Sodo-san had no choice but to follow, even if he didn't formulate the feeling in his mind, and that was the authority of his own heart.

When Dogen returned to Japan after arriving at his understanding of the Buddhist Way as a result of his years in China, he taught a way that threatened the powerful Buddhist institutions of his time. He fled the then–Buddhist capital in Japan, fearing for his life as well as protecting a teaching he refused to abandon. It was his creative understanding of Zen practice, and though he phrased it in the words of one following the way of his Chinese master Ju-ching, it was, in fact, Dogen's way.

Kodo Sawaki, too, followed his own way, though he professed to be expressing the teachings of Dogen. Truly creative teachers can do nothing else. So it was with other great teachers like Hakuin and Bankei, to name two from the other major Zen sect in Japan. What eventually happens, once institutions are formed to follow the ways of these masters, is a slow decline of the original spirit and a dependence on forms and dogmas that water down the true teaching of the founders.

I believe that institutions of Zen no longer express the true spirit of zazen. Zazen is independent of all things, including zazen itself. Sodo-san may not have agreed with the way I describe the practice, but there was something inside him that expressed that very idea, and drove him to move to Komoro and live the life he chose. One feels it not only in his life under the stars at Kaikoen Park, but in his extensive writing on zazen.

From left to right: Kyuji Inoue, Sodo-san, Joko (serving lunch), and the daughter (barely shown) of one of Sodo-san's admirers

8

Sodo-san, the Twentieth-Century Ryokan

In an interview with Joko at our first meeting in 1995, I recall him shocking me by saying he felt responsible for his teacher's early death (age seventy-four is only early when compared with Sawaki's and Uchiyama's deaths at eighty-five). Despite the testimony by a visiting reporter for the Buddhist Publisher, Daihorin, who shared one of Joko's meals with him and Sodo-san, and raved about Joko's cooking, Joko insisted he could have given his teacher more nutritious fare.

Joko pooh-poohed the praise of his cooking, saying, "Of course he would say that. Wouldn't you if you were a guest at someone's house?" And added, "I have my regrets." He went on to talk about the life of poverty his teacher chose. "My teacher used to go to the park during the coldest part of winter. Little by little he exhausted all his energy. He lived with the bare minimum—in poverty. In fact, he perfected this life of poverty."

Here, I am reminded once more of the monk Sodo-san

often referred to as a model to give meaning to his own choice of lifestyle, Taigu Ryokan. There were many differences in the lives of Ryokan-san and Sodo-san, but they really don't concern me. What is important is what Sodo-san saw in this gentle monk who lived 150 years before him, the characteristics in Ryokan with which he identified. Neither monk was suited to involve himself in the family business, both trained in Soto Zen Buddhist monasteries, both loved poetry and calligraphy, and both enjoyed the company of children.

People loved Ryokan-san for what he brought to *their* lives, and not necessarily for who *he* actually was. For how can we separate the myth from the man? And how important is it to do so? He gave us someone to love and a reason to believe. That's why people refer to him as Ryokan-san (Mr. Ryokan) and not Zen Master Ryokan. He brought Buddhism to the world of everyday people in Japan. His simple life and his wise advice taught people how to look at their own lives. He was more like a wise uncle than a Zen master. His wisdom did not feel like it came from someone standing on high ground, but rather from one who suffered the human predicament as we all do.

Sodo-san may never reach the mythic proportions of Ryokan-san, but he symbolizes for me a monk of the people. His calligraphy is delicate like Ryokan's; and his poetry, like Ryokan's, is very personal; and, most importantly, like Ryokan-san, he truly came alive in the presence of children.

*A lone monk begging in the streets of Kyoto from 1949
to 1957 would suddenly take a leaf from a tree and put
it to his mouth. Then you would hear the beginning of
an unimaginably beautiful tune. You might see him
leading a group of children, all walking in tune to the
leaf playing—just like the Pied Piper of Hamelin. . . .
While children happily gathered around this monk, as
children did around Ryokan one hundred fifty years ago,
he would suddenly cover his head with the wide black
sleeve of his monk's robe, and the children would run
away squealing in delicious fear. . . . This monk was
called the "Leaf-whistle Player" throughout Kyoto. He
is my elder-brother disciple. . . .*

The above was taken from an article written by Kosho
Uchiyama, the then-abbot of Antaiji, on August 22, 1968.
He and Sodo-san lived together at Antaiji from 1949 until
Sodo-san decided to move to Komoro City and spend his
remaining days in the park following his heart.

In Sodo-san's writings, he refers to Ryokan-san as the true
representative of the *Yamato* spirit. *Yamato* was the original
name for Japan, the Japan before the influence of China. The
word represents the beauty and the ugliness in Japanese history, but for Sodo-san it is the beauty. His oft-brushed poem
was of a famous piece that Ryokan composed in response to
a woman who asked him for a keepsake:

What shall I leave as a keepsake?
cherry blossoms in spring
the warbler's song in summer
crimson leaves of the maple in autumn.

I feel that Ryokan's love of nature is only part of what Sodo-san identifies with in this ancient Zen man as the *Yamato* spirit. While Zen represents the way of the warrior for many in Japan, there is another side to Zen expressed more in the Soto school than the other major Zen sect, Rinzai. It is seen in the Pure Land schools, particularly the Jodo Shin Pure Land sect of Japan: the belief that we are deluded individuals saved by the vow of Amida Buddha. Both monks felt incapable of being in charge of a monastery. They felt a weakness inside themselves, but a strength in the fact that they are saved despite their weakness.

Ryokan-san famously brushed:

What a joy to realize
because I am a hopeless soul
I've found Amida Buddha's vow.

Sodo-san also felt saved by a force greater than himself. For him, *shikantaza* (Dogen's words for what Shunryu Suzuki translates as 'just sitting') is what Amida's vow is to Ryokan. He brushed many poems in praise of this form of zazen.

If there is one
who discards this world
it is shikantaza *alone*
that actually does the discarding.

What I gather from the personality of these two Zen men is a softness rarely associated with Zen Buddhism. It is a major component of the *Yamato* spirit in Sodo-san's eyes, at least. I think of it as the feminine side of Zen—the quality of *aware,* a term that has many meanings, 'intense feelings' being the most general. It was a common sentiment in early Japanese literature and came to carry a feeling of sadness and even tragedy.

There is another term that I associate with both monks, a word that carries the meaning of an 'artistic style' or 'elegance' but to me it feels more like 'funky.' The Japanese is *furyu.* In the hands of the most famous Japanese tea master, Sen no Rikyu, it would carry the meaning of 'elegant simplicity.'

I believe I read it in John Stevens's account of Ryokan where he tells of a relative of Ryokan's request that he speak to the man's delinquent son to encourage him to mend his troublesome ways. Ryokan stayed the night at his relative's house watching the son but not saying a word of admonishment. The following morning when the boy was tying Ryokan's sandals (a respectful way when seeing an elder off) he felt drops of warm water drip on his shoulders. He looked up and saw tears in Ryokan's eyes. Later it was said that the boy's behavior improved from that day. Whether this was myth or fact, it expresses another quality in this gentle monk that attracted Sodo-san.

Taigu Ryokan with his begging bowl

9

Sodo-san's Temple Under the Sky

Why does the practice of zazen feel more like getting into Buddhism than *takuhatsu* (the Japanese word for a religious mendicancy practice)? Is it an American thing? Like weeding at a monastery? When I lived at Antaiji, I remember one of the monks asking me why Americans like big jobs like chopping wood but eschew work like weeding. I feel it has something to do with Americans living in Zen monasteries being a lot more full of themselves, or full of the idea of becoming enlightened, than Japanese. The image of "me chopping wood" is large, but "me weeding," well . . .

I went on *takuhatsu* with the Antaiji monks and all I can remember was being glad when it was over. But zazen? That was the real thing. That was the road to enlightenment. I'm embarrassed remembering that feeling, but I can't deny it. Even though my knees ached and my back hurt when I sat in zazen, meditation carried the image of taking part in the 'real' Buddha activity. I don't think the Japanese monks had the feeling of being an individual on the path to the degree that we Westerners did. For them, doing what the group was doing at the time was more important; some probably thought of it as 'Buddha activity.'

Like Ryokan-san, Sodo-san had practiced *takuhatsu*. He practiced it during his years at Antaiji. Unlike Ryokan, he didn't continue the practice when he arrived at Kaikoen in Komoro. I asked Joko why his teacher didn't continue this practice. It was, after all, an age-old custom, and still a part of Zen training monasteries.

"Leaf-playing was his *takuhatsu*," Joko said.

It's true that people gave Sodo-san money when he played a tune on the leaf, and that he thanked them with calligraphy that he brushed on the spot, but I wondered whether there might be more to it than Joko's explanation.

Sodo-san followed his own way with the independence of a true artist. Not an easy thing for a monk in twentieth-century Japan. He might have fit in better as an ancient Taoist master in China. His zazen was the meditation of a truly independent monk. It was based on the zazen taught by his teacher, Kodo Sawaki, a practice rarely found in twentieth-century monasteries in Japan.

Kodo Sawaki often railed against what he referred to as 'group stupidity.' He said he did zazen to be free of that group stupidity. I'm sure young Sodo-san was attracted to a teaching in which one was given license to do his own thing. Sawaki often talked about the purity of zazen. He very clearly distinguished it from what he called ordinary life:

"*. . . you are using your mind to figure things out—how*
to get through this world in a better fashion, how to
make money, how to move up in the world, how to make
life easier, how to make it more pleasurable . . . zazen,"
he added, "puts all that aside . . ."

How exciting a teaching like that must have sounded to
a young man who had no desire to join the world of name
and fame. To a young man who loved to watch the sunset, to
write verse, and play the leaf. To a young artist who felt truly
out of touch with the fast-paced world around him.

Sodo-san did not feel above those who chose to live in
the ordinary world. Like Ryokan, he truly seemed to feel
inadequate to compete in that world. To accept one's inad-
equacies was a major aspect of the type of zazen Sawaki
preached. But there was another side to that zazen that may
have appealed to Sodo-san on a different level. Practical as
Sawaki was when he recommended zazen, he also talked
about the practice with a reverence for it that raised it to
heights one might see as magical. You were not expected to
do anything, just to sit and let zazen do its thing. It shone on
all regardless of station in the world, as did the sun.

"Many years ago, I'd fallen in love with the evening sky,"
Sodo-san wrote. "I'd stand on the peak of Konzan Mountain and gaze at the sky at the close of each day. No matter
how cloudy it was, as long as it wasn't raining or snowing
I would stand on the mountain gazing at the sky. However

beautiful this evening sky was, at the end of the day the sun would sink and the evening sky would disappear in the darkness. Had the sun never sunk, and the evening sky remained visible, I feel I would have become crazy, never leaving it out of my sight. But as beautiful as the evening sky was, it would eventually disappear into the darkness and I would feel relieved as I descended the mountain. One evening, I realized that the evening sun was giving me a hint into the meaning 'all things {are like} scattered thoughts.'" Then he made the jump to "The sunset doesn't know it's the sunset, but it is the sunset. And as with the sunset, all things are like disappearing thoughts."

This was to inform his understanding of Sawaki's zazen, and make him declare that zazen was the only thing that was safe (in baseball terms). In zazen there was no birth and no death. Everything was as it is. He could be who he was and not concern himself with feelings of inferiority or superiority. He would sit in the park and practice zazen and play his music and be an example of one who practiced the Way, letting go of thoughts and having exchanges with people, as Ryokan did when he was out on *takuhatsu*.

Like so many artists, Sodo-san was basically a shy man. When people wanted to learn something about zazen, however, like his disciple, Joko, he could talk your ear off. He told Kyuji Inoue, the reporter for Daihorin Buddhist Publishing Group who visited Sodo-san at the park, that it took six or seven years to decide on the spot to set up his Temple Under the Sky. He said he first sat under a pine tree and

Joko Shibata sitting zazen in the meditation hall he built in memory
of his teacher

played his leaf, then moved around until he found the place that felt right to him. I feel that was a condensed version of his life. Practicing in monasteries, following his teacher's suggestions, until he arrived at the place he wanted to be, doing what he loved. A life that he would refer to as an easy one.

10

Zazen Is Safe. This Life Is Easy.

When I first met Joko years after his teacher's death, he was living in a house he'd purchased about a half–hour's drive from Kaikoen Park. He'd built a small zendo (a Zen meditation room) onto the house with the money he saved from years of working at a miso factory.

"My teacher dreamed of building a meditation hall when he retired from his practice at the park (he considered his life at the park an extension of his Zen practice) but he never got the chance," Joko said. "So I decided to do it for him."

Joko has been living in that house since his teacher's death, practicing zazen, studying the works of Sodo-san, Kodo Sawaki (his teacher's teacher), and the writings of Zen Master Dogen. His daily meditation when I first met him consisted of at least ten fifty-minute sittings, far more hours than sat the two teachers he virtually worshipped.

I couldn't help but wonder whether the extreme devotion to the words of his predecessors, which apparently drove him to such extremes of practice, might have some hidden reason behind it. I love the practice myself, but both Sodo-san and Sawaki Roshi seemed to have a more rounded life than that of 'just sitting.' They preached the importance of zazen practice while expressing it in their lives in other ways besides sitting meditation. Could one hide behind the practice of zazen? Or is it just my inherent skepticism that doesn't allow me to simply accept the fact that Joko's love of zazen and of his teachers are the sole reasons he embraced the practice to such an extent?

I'd often debated with Joko about some of Kodo Sawaki's teachings, but I didn't feel it was my place to present him with my doubts about his own practice. Not until I got to know him better. Not until he would trust that I wasn't saying it to criticize him but rather to enquire together. I was curious, however, about his practice during the time he attended to Sodo-san, so I asked him.

"Where did you live when you moved to Komoro after training at Eiheiji Monastery?"

"I rented a room in the same boardinghouse as my teacher. I lived on the first floor and he on the second."

"What was your daily schedule like then?"

"We sat zazen together at five each morning for fifty minutes. Then I prepared breakfast, we ate, and I went off to work. When I returned home, we ate dinner together at seven o'clock, cleaned up, and then Roshi talked with me about Buddhism until nine."

One fifty-minute sitting a day. A guy who sits ten fifty-minute sittings now that his teacher is gone. Was he content to have meditated only fifty minutes a day so that he could be around his teacher? Does he meditate so much now in order to feel close to the teacher who talked about zazen as though it were the one thing that made life worthwhile? Questions too abstract to tackle with Joko now. I will have to, sometime, if my investigation into the world of Sodo-san is to be as complete as I can make it.

"Zazen is safe." That statement is one I will have to come back to throughout my attempts to understand the Grass Flute Zen Master. That and the statement "This life is easy." Easy for Sodo-san or easy for the Universe? Does life have to be a struggle if one is to help others? Something tells me that when it works for the Universe, it only looks like a struggle from the outside.

The real struggle I imagine Sodo-san had, as did his hero Ryokan, was living in a community that required him to follow the group—read sutras at a specific time, beg with the group, and in many more ways follow the leader. Not that those rules and instructions do not have value for the many, especially when they are rules set down by wise men, but for those few who feel a calling from inside them, the group practice can be suffocating.

When Sodo-san proclaimed zazen as 'safe' he was referring to zazen as taught by Kodo Sawaki. It is a zazen that, as I wrote before when quoting Sawaki, takes a break from the human world. It takes a break from "the world of wanting money, wanting to taste good food, wanting things to be easy. . . ." It helps one escape the world in which people "spend their lives seeking sex, food, position . . ."—a world in which we "think in terms of good or bad or judge right from wrong. . . ."

What a relief this kind of zazen is for someone who has felt himself viewing the world differently from those around him. To be allowed to follow your heart and not to follow the rules of the masses, to be given license to *be who you are*.

For years, Sodo-san studied with people who would give him a better understanding of his teacher's zazen, all the while feeling he was getting a clearer message from the Buddha within. As time went on, he developed more confidence in that internal voice, which eventually pushed him to make

From left to right: Kyuji Inoue, daughter of a fan of Sodo-san, Sodo Yokoyama, and Joko Shibata practicing zazen

the break. Once that break was made, he felt his life became 'easy.'

When Kyuji Inoue of Daihorin visited Sodo-san at the park for the second day, a young woman sat on the spot he'd previously occupied. She'd come from Ibaragi Prefecture.

"This young princess brought me this," Sodo-san said, showing Inoue a cotton-padded jacket he was wearing. The woman explained to Inoue that her mother had woven it on her loom for Roshi's seventieth birthday. She said her father was a Soto Zen priest who had temple duties that didn't allow him to live like Sodo-san. She added, "My mother said 'there is no purer monk than Sodo-san.'"

Sodo-san's 'easy life' must have appeared differently to each of the many people who came upon him sitting in the park playing his leaf or doing zazen. But I doubt there were many who considered it an easy life.

Sodo-san with elementary school students at the park

11

Forever Young

My fondest memory is when we visited Kaikoen Park and that man played the "Song of a Traveler's Weary Heart by Chikuma River" on the leaf. He taught us, playing it over and over until we got good at it. He played the song and sang it to us and showed us how to play the leaf. He didn't give up on us though we knew nothing [about playing the leaf]. It is the one memory in my life as an elementary school student that I will never forget. We sang it on our way to school and on our way home—the song that kind man taught us about the old castle in Komoro, and the white clouds and a lonely traveler . . .

—Setsuko Nakano, sixth grader

Always a kid. Always an amateur. Those were Sodo-san's sentiments. He is the oldest, wisest kid I've ever met. He loved his amateur status because it allowed him to be who he was and not who people thought he should be.

"When you play the leaf," he once wrote, "you'll usually be a little out of tune. That's where its very charm lies. . . ."

As Shunryu Suzuki famously said, "In the beginner's mind there are many possibilities, but in the expert's there are few."

Substitute 'amateur' for 'beginner,' and you have Sodo-san's philosophy.

When Steve, Lew, and I visited Sodo-san at the park in 1970, a lady came up to him and asked his age.

"Nineteen," he said.

She had an uncomfortable smile, like she didn't know how to respond, and so didn't say anything else. She didn't ask him to play a tune for her, and I imagine his answer to her question about his age and the three foreigners he'd been talking with were intimidating to her.

I remember, at the time, wondering whether Sodo-san was annoyed with the question or simply being sarcastic. But when I was able to read some of his writing a year later I realized it was neither.

On a scroll, beautifully brushed, is a piece titled "Nineteen Springs." He writes about moving to Kaikoen Park in his fifty-second year, and how, after ten years playing his compositions and meditating in the park, people started to refer to him as 'grandpa.'

"Not even in my dreams," he brushed some years later, "do I think of myself as a grandpa. The grass flute is never blown by grown-ups or old people. It is the play of children.

When kids grow up they forget about their childhood play and about blowing sounds on the grass flute. It is for the mind of a child. . . ."

If Sodo-san was teaching the Dharma to travelers in the park, it was the dharma of staying young at heart. He said he would like to tell people he is fourteen when they ask, but they wouldn't believe him, so he said nineteen. And he told older people when they came to hear him play the grass flute that they, too, must also become nineteen (again). He was gratified when older tourists told him that he made their day, allowing them to forget the woes of old age. That kind of response made him feel he was preforming a service to the small circle of travelers in the park.

But there is more behind this lifestyle of his than simply to make old folks feel young. When he felt his enthusiasm for spiritual practice wane as he got older, he felt that he had to learn not to let age defeat him.

In "The Woods Where I Stand" (我が立つそま) Sodo-san writes, "At age twenty-two or twenty-three one is at the peak of his spiritual consciousness. After that, spiritual consciousness starts to wane." He goes on to say that you learn worldly things as you grow older, but the "original face of the Universal life is something apart from what you can see or conceive. But you do intuit it." He added that all people in their youth intuit the Universe.

Sodo-san uses the word 'Universe' to mean the cosmos or the unity of all things. He feels that if a young person were to come in contact with zazen when he or she intuits the Universe, that person would be able to hold onto that intuitive feeling and maintain his or her youthful grasp of the spirit.

I try to understand Sodo-san's message about remaining young, though I find it difficult. I remember traveling through the Far East on a spiritual quest in my twenties and certainly do recall the excitement, which is perhaps lost to some extent as I face old age. That excitement was accompanied by some restlessness, which I don't welcome back. Maybe one can maintain a youthful excitement in old age without the restlessness that accompanied it in youth.

When I recall seeing Sodo-san in the park and at the yearly memorials for Kodo Sawaki, I remember a man who did seem to possess that youthfulness while being quite at ease with himself.

I can still hear Sodo-san welcoming Kyuji Inoue to his bamboo grove in the park when he was in his seventieth year.

"Please take off your shoes and sit down," he said, welcoming the reporter. "This is my dragon castle, and I'm Urashima Taro."

Urashima Taro is a young fisherman from an old Japanese folktale. He was led to a dragon castle beneath the sea and returned to the world on land hundreds of years later, still a young man (until he blew it by opening a jeweled hand box given to him by a princess with instruction never to open).

Sodo-san's dragon castle consisted of flattened cardboard boxes with cushions on top, a cooker on top of a pile of earth (to allow water to drain off when it rained), two areas near some bamboo clumps lined with sheets of old corrugated plastic and tin, and various pieces of equipment packed together. And, of course, his bowl with leaves in water. When a guest visited, Sodo-san would take a piece of cardboard and a mat from what Mr. Inoue described as a personal locker and place it for the guest to sit. The locker also stored various knickknacks used for cooking. This was Sodo-san's world for the last twenty-two years of his life.

As he described it to Mr. Inoue, "All you have to do is decide that wherever you are is the best place there is. Once you start comparing one place to another, there is no end to it." Inoue likened Sodo-san's dragon castle to a children's playhouse. That playhouse was the home of a very mature monk whose practice of zazen seems to have kept him young while giving him wisdom.

Sodo-san meditating in the park

12

I saw zazen as a posture bestowed
upon me by the Buddha.
—SODO YOKOYAMA

Joko gave me many examples of his teacher's beautiful calligraphy, which I treasure. His style resembles that of Ryokan's but with a more polished look. Not to say that that makes it better or worse, just different. It may be partly due to the better brushes Sodo-san had to work with, and partly to the different lifestyles and personalities of the two men.

On his visit to Sodo-san in the park, Kyuji Inoue wrote of his regret at missing an exchange he'd heard about between Sodo-san and some visitors. When people gave Sodo-san a contribution after hearing him play a tune on the leaf, he would thank them with a calligraphy he'd brush on the spot. The ones I have were probably brushed sometime in his room, for they seem to show the care its author could only give to his work by a bench in an atmosphere of tranquility.

Long before I met Joko, an Antaiji monk named Koshi Ichida gave me two of Sodo-san's calligraphies after visiting him at the park. Koshi was to leave for America at Kosho Uchiyama's request. Many other people connected with Antaiji, including its abbot, visited Sodo-san in the park, and he was always happy to see people from his old stomping ground show up there.

Though Sodo-san left Antaiji to continue his practice by following his heart, his connection to the monastery stayed with him his whole life. Many of his poems and songs depict his life while training at Antaiji.

Near the eave's edge of Antaiji's shrine
Sasanqua bloom
Their petals scatter on the veranda.

The roof
damaged from the storm
The bush clover
in Antaiji's garden
is peaceful.

So why did Sodo-san leave Antaiji? There are many possible answers to that question, and some of them partly true. One, I mentioned earlier, was a need to express himself freely, to follow his heart, which included a certain amount of what Walt Whitman called "loafing." There is no place for loafing in a Japanese monastery. There is no place for loafing in Japanese society, period. And, I believe, poets need time to loaf. They are dreamers, and can find it as difficult to be with their family as to be with monks at a monastery—to be with a majority of non-dreamers, who have little sympathy for them.

Sodo-san's father and his teacher, Kodo Sawaki, seemed to have understood what he needed. His father introduced him to zazen and Sawaki helped him refine it. Though his unusual life as a leaf-blowing poet, musician, and calligrapher are what made him unique enough to write a story about, it was his love of zazen that became the core of his existence.

"One spring evening," he wrote, "when I was seven, my father sat by the sliding paper doors and playfully showed me the zazen posture. 'The Buddha practiced this way,' he said. In my young mind, the Buddha [was a fellow who] practiced like my dad. . . ."

Sodo-san's father was a learned man, who cautioned his son about being deceived by the belief that acquiring rational knowledge is wisdom. His father paved the way for Sodo-san to appreciate the zazen of Sawaki.

The rational mind wants to gain something from the experience of meditation. Sawaki's zazen is the teaching of no-gain. For Sodo-san to hear that one practices leaving all to zazen was a relief. He was given permission to be himself and not feel he had to compete. Like Ryokan, he felt incapable of competing in the world. Zazen gave him the license to let those who want to move up in the world to do so, while he would just sit and enjoy the blessings of the universe.

I don't mean to suggest that Sodo-san was a taker and not

a giver. He did what he believed to be true zazen and people could feel that faith when they came in contact with him. He was an inspiration to the travelers in the park, to those who watched on TV when NHK did a program on him, and to many, like myself, now that he is gone. He taught us by needing little and being content with his life. Zazen for Sodo-san was like Arunachala, the hill in Tiruvannamalai, was to the Indian saint Ramana Maharshi, a truth beyond thought—the only true realization.

When Sodo-san chose Ryokan as a role model for his solitary way of life, he wrote: "When I thought about who I was, I realized that I could never be a respectable man of the world. If I couldn't be a respectable man of the world, I couldn't be a respectable monk either. That's why I never considered being a Zen teacher."

He did, however, become a monk. He added: "I saw zazen as 'a posture bestowed upon me by the Buddha.' The myriad things then became, 'beyond thought' and home became a sacred place. . . . Whether people of the world practiced it or not, zazen is the [true] way of the world, the way of the universe. . . ." He went on to say that he did have a duty to pass this practice of zazen to others and that he would do it by sitting in Kaikoen Park where people would see him and some among them would show an interest in the practice. He said that he would have to keep the practice himself first, and, quoting his teacher, "Make an offering of your body to zazen."

So he chose to teach in the only way he felt capable, to

offer his body to zazen. People were drawn to this lone monk who sat in the park and played songs on the leaf at their request. To many he was a curiosity, a street performer of a unique kind. To some, however, like the mother of the girl who weaved him a coat so he wouldn't freeze in the cold Komoro winters, he was a monk of the truest kind. He represented a world that was disappearing in Japan. Others started a Grass Flute group who, since Sodo-san's death, have met at the park every Sunday to play songs on the leaf. But most importantly, to some he was the embodiment of meditation, and they were encouraged to practice.

Among the last group was Joko. He'd chosen the way of zazen before he ever knew Sodo-san. He joined Antaiji after graduating college. Despite the intense practice at Antaiji, Joko felt something unsatisfying. When Sodo-san came to Antaiji for the annual memorial ceremony for Sawaki Roshi, Joko gazed upon him in zazen posture. That changed his life. In his words, he could see the truth of the practice in the posture of Sodo-san.

"I could tell just from seeing him, and I knew I wanted to be his disciple," Joko said.

His life has been devoted to his teacher ever since.

There are many stories of devoted disciples who have brought us the teaching of their masters, important teaching that may not have come down to us if these disciples hadn't given of themselves completely to their masters. Koun Ejo, the dharma heir of Zen Master Dogen, is one such disciple. Ejo's record of Dogen's informal talks, *Zuimonki*, is the most accessible of Dogen's instructions. It was a book that came into Sodo-san's hands when he was twenty-two. While working for his brother who was in charge of the family weaving business, he read the *Zuimonki* over and over and resolved to practice zazen.

Sodo-san's teaching comes to us solely because of the devotional work of Joko. Joko brings us his teacher's music and poetry as well as his writings on zazen. He is no musician, poet, or calligrapher, but he practices zazen with a passion not even his teacher could match.

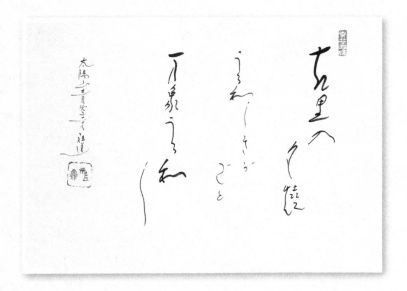

The sunset of my hometown
is as beautiful as
the beauty of all phenomena.

—Sodo, from *The Sun Mountain, Temple Under the Sky*

13

The Poet of *Leaves of Grass*
and the Grass Flute Zen Master

I'm riding with Mr. Iwazawa. He's giving me a lift to the Saku Station, the closest Bullet Train station from Komoro. He helped Joko transform Sodo-san's music into an electronic format. Joko wants to do whatever he can to spread his teacher's work. I don't think he can see how any instrument other than the leaf will destroy the spirit (and uniqueness) of his teacher's music.

Mr. Iwazawa, who oversaw the publishing of a handsome book of Sodo-san's photos, poems, and calligraphy, surprises me when he says he never met the man.

"We published the book a year after Yokoyama Roshi died."

"How did you get involved?" I ask.

"My older sister is married to Yokoyama Roshi's nephew."

It's interesting to me how many people who never met the man are influenced by Sodo-san, like many from the group that meets in Kaikoen Park every Sunday to play the leaf.

"What kind of music interests you?" I ask Iwazawa, having realized from our previous conversation that it wasn't zazen that intrigued him about Sodo-san, and wondering if he was interested in the music. He must have thought I meant American music because he said, "Country-Western."

When I met Sodo-san in the park he'd said to us that he liked Stephen Foster. As I mentioned earlier, he played "Old Folks at Home" when he saw three foreigners approaching. He told us on our visit that day that he also loved Walt Whitman. Neither Joko nor Mr. Iwazawa had any idea that Sodo-san was interested in the famous composer or the great American Bard.

I'd wanted to make the trip to Kaikoen Park in 1970 because I fantasized he would be someone like the Indian Saint Ramana Maharshi. The Maharshi sat in a cave on a mountainside absorbed in "god consciousness" for many years and lived on that mountain for the rest of his life. Before I was informed otherwise, I'd thought Sodo-san lived in the park. I was disappointed at first to learn that he lived in a boarding-house and spent his days in the park.

Sodo-san was no Maharshi, but he satisfied my need to find a Japanese monk who lived the life of an ideal man of Zen. When Sodo-san told us he loved Walt Whitman, my favorite American man of letters, I knew he wouldn't disappoint me.

There is nothing in Sodo-san's writing about Whitman, so all I have is that one statement when we met in the park. Whitman's writings are often mistaken (in my opinion) as those of an American nationalist, a spokesman for the American ideal of democracy. I believe they are really about the author's personal experience of a oneness of nature. Something he must have experienced, and sprouted forth in him as a great American poem. The 'I' in his "Song of Myself" (a title that was attached to the poem long after his first edition) is not a personal I. It is the 'I' of a mystical, democratic soul. I see in Sodo-san's expression of the *Yamato* man, not an ancient Japanese—to which *Yamato* is usually attributed—but rather to the spirit of zazen in all men.

Like those who interpreted Whitman as a patriot when reading only small sections of his writing, one can mistakenly interpret Sodo-san's writing as patriotic or nationalistic. But patriots and nationalists are usually ambitious. Sodo-san, like Whitman, would prefer, as the bard wrote, to ". . . loaf and invite my soul/I lean and loaf at my ease . . . observing a spear of summer grass . . ." (in Sodo-san's case, "a leaf of summer grass").

Sodo-san chose to sit in a public park, demonstrating for all women and men who happened to pass by that zazen is for everyone who wishes to try. I think he also believed that it influences all regardless of whether they choose to practice it formally or not.

It is impossible to know how thoroughly Sodo-san read Whitman, but if he had read "Song of Myself," Part Six would have resonated with him on many levels. "A child said, What is the grass? fetching it to me with full hands; How could I

answer the child . . . I do not know what it is any more than
he . . ." And Whitman goes on to present many images that he
guesses the grass to be.

Whether Sodo-san thought about the leaves he produced
music from to be like the world of images Whitman describes,
I'm sure Whitman's images would have excited him. And the
statement "I do not know what it is any more than he" would
resonate with Sodo-san's view of zazen—a practice that cannot be expressed in words, and doesn't require knowing. In
fact, I might add, can never be known.

Much more can be said of parallels between Whitman's
"Song of Myself" and Sodo-san's writings on zazen, but it
would begin to sound like a critique of Whitman and not, as
I intended, a look at Sodo-san, the man and his works. There
is, however, one more thing to be said, something essential
to understanding these two poets. Whitman's first edition of
Leaves of Grass appears to be a result of the author's profound
mystical experience. And, as the critic Malcolm Cowley suggests, every new edition gives one the feeling that Whitman's
growing distance from that experience results in a more
self-conscious and less authentic version of what has to be
one of the most unique poems in America's literary history.

Sodo-san's experience, in the mountain near his hometown, of watching the sun and feeling that if it didn't sink in
the sky he would never be able to tear himself away from gazing at it, was, for him, a profound mystical experience. Unlike
Whitman, he realized that as he got older his spiritual awareness would lose its original power. Also, unlike Whitman, he

had a practice, zazen, that would at least keep him from being blind to that fact. For him, zazen was his way of returning as much as possible to that original experience.

Walt Whitman, age thirty-five, from the frontispiece of *Leaves of Grass*, steel engraving by Samuel Hollyer

14

The Gentle Poet Preaching His Silent Sermon in the Park

I am much more comfortable writing about what Sodo-san may have found to resonate with in Whitman than I am with what he took from the masters of Japanese poetry, whether it be *haiku* or *waka*. Though I don't think he ever formally studied *haiku*, in his youth he did have discussions about the form with a friend who studied with a master. In "The Woods Where I Stand" (我が立つそま) he stated that one who didn't study Basho, the famed *haiku* poet, could never create true poetry. He added that the tradition handed down by Basho allowed one to see the beauty in Japan, in the world, and in the universe.

Masaoka Shiki (1867–1902), the founder of the *shasei* (sketching from nature) poetry movement, who was critical of *haiku* poets' imitating the old masters, composed *haiku* and *waka* poetry that gave poets who came after him, including Sodo-san, the freedom to express themselves in

ways that would not have been accepted before Shiki's rev-
olutionary ideas. (Ryokan, whose poetry seemed to be free
of any imitation, may have been the exception, and may not
have been well known in poetry circles during Shiki's time.)

Why Sodo-san composed *waka* and not *haiku*, consider-
ing friends in his youth studied and talked about *haiku,* is
surprising. However, *haiku,* the shorter of the two poetic
styles—consisting of only three lines, 5-7-5 syllables (*waka*
consists of five lines, 5-7-5-7-7)—does not leave much space
for the poet to express anything more than a fleeting impression of something seen or felt. Like Ryokan, Whitman, and
Shiki, Sodo-san needed to express himself in his own way
and the *waka*, though short by Western standards, allowed
him to put more of himself in his poems than *haiku*. It also
may have been easier to adapt for his songs.

I read in one of the Whitman biographies that he considered traveling around the country reciting his poetry in
order to bring the message to the masses. His poetry was
his religion and he was passionate about spreading the word.
There certainly is a tradition of traveling preachers in both
America and Japan.

Kodo Sawaki, Sodo-san's Zen teacher, traveled the country most of his days giving talks to laypeople and monks
alike. Like Sodo-san, Sawaki wanted to tell people the 'good
news' about zazen.

Sodo-san, too shy to preach on street corners or at temples, set up his Temple Under the Sky in a corner of the park

and preached his silent sermon. When someone asked him to play his music or sing his songs, he accommodated, but his main message was zazen.

In the poem quoted below, the possessive pronoun "my" is absent in the Japanese:

> *Years ago*
> *meditating in the mountains*
> *a pheasant appeared*
> *and stared*
> *at my zazen.*

"My" is understood, and I put it in to clarify the image. Sodo-san, like his teacher, does not think of zazen as something *he* is doing. Zazen does zazen, and that's why the pheasant is not frightened by the person. Sodo-san has given himself up to zazen. He could not express that idea in a form as brief and as objective as *haiku*. Why? Let's look at Basho's most famous *haiku:*

> *An ancient pond*
> *A frog jumps in*
> *Splash!*

There is no Basho in this scene.

Though Sodo-san disappears into zazen, the pheasant teaches him, by showing no fear. It is not as immediate as

Matsuo Basho

Basho's frog poem because it involves a lesson upon reflection. Sodo-san has been taught by the pheasant's sensitivity how powerful and yet peaceful zazen can be.

While Basho's frog *haiku* shows the immediacy of the moment, Sodo-san's *waka* is an expression of an ongoing awareness of the depth of zazen. Most of his poems are not so directly about zazen—how much can one say about a practice of just sitting. As I reflect on the frog *haiku*, I realize that it can be seen as an aspect of the same zazen.

Masaoka Shiki brought everyday language into his poetry, a must in his estimation for the poem to be genuine. He loved baseball and liked to shock the traditionalists by even putting baseball in nine of his *waka*. One example:

The bases are full
Men of the other team
On all three bases;
In spite of myself I feel
My heart pound with emotion.

—translated by Donald Keene

Sodo-san was a fan of baseball as a child and wrote about it in his prose reflections, but left it out of his poems. He composed *waka* about the death of family members, his life at Antaiji, begging, the beauty of the sunset, children, his hometown, and many more subjects. Some fit nicely into the tradition of the ancients like the following:

Sasanqua flowers
bloom again this year
near Antaiji's shrine
Pigeons fly away.

Two poems he brushed for Kosho Uchiyama, when the abbot of Antaiji visited him at the park, reflect the complicated feelings of a 'home-leaver,' the epithet for a monk:

Mother and Father
Brothers and Sisters
Forgive me
A child without a home.

More than mother
More than father
More than brothers and sisters
I love the mountains and rivers
How pitiful!

The two longtime disciples of Kodo Sawaki had spent many years together at Antaiji taking care of the temple in Sawaki's absence. I imagine they talked about their reasons for shaving their heads. For Uchiyama it was after the death of his second wife. He was falling apart emotionally and entered a temple at the insistence of his father. Sodo-san's decision may have been made without consultation with his family. In his prose writing he expressed his feeling of being inadequate to function as a householder. He brushed the above poems for his brother disciple of Kodo Sawaki because he knew Uchiyama would understand.

In director Akira Kurosawa's masterpiece, the movie *Kagemusha* ("The Double"), the leaders of two rival clans are at war. When Oda Nobunaga learns that his rival Takeda Shingen has been killed, he has conflicting feelings. He is happy because it means his clan will lead Japan, but he also feels respect for his brave rival who has fallen. His response is to do a traditional dance that expresses both joy and pathos.

At first I thought it a strange reaction on Nobunaga's part. But on reflection I realized that a society where one's deportment is so important, expressing one's feelings in a beautiful art form would be more acceptable than to scream it out as we from the West might do. For Sodo-san, personal feelings were better expressed in poems and songs.

15

My Teacher Perfected a Life of Poverty

Sitting zazen daily in the park earned Sodo-san the respect of lay and monastic practitioners. His beautiful calligraphy and his fine poetry may not have been so rare from a monk who traced his family lineage to retainers to the shogun of ancient Japan. Many abbots of major temples in Japan also were expected to brush and compose poetry. But a lone monk spending his days in a bamboo grove meditating, brushing poems and songs, and playing those musical compositions on a leaf—that was unique. Most of all, it was his music, and the funky way he brought it to the public that made him a celebrity of Kaikoen Park.

There were, of course, the *komuso,* a sect of Zen Buddhists who trace their history back to thirteenth-century Japan, who play the bamboo flute. They flourished during the Edo period (1600–1868). They wore straw hats that covered their faces and played the *shakuhachi* (a bamboo flute) as part of their meditative practice. The Meiji government abolished their sect (the Fuke sect) because there was a history of spies disguised as *komuso* during periods of unrest in Japan. There is a revival of their music in Japan today.

If Sodo-san was trying to revive a history, it was the history of his childhood. I imagine his childhood must have been joyful, and that he wanted to hold onto it. When I was translating the teaching of Suzuki Shosan (the ex-samurai monk), A Japanese monk friend of mine—whom I greatly respect—looked over Shosan's writing. When he came across one of Shosan's talks, he said, "This is the most important section." Shosan had said, "Remember the feeling of your childhood, how you played in the rain and snow, thinking, Ah, what fun! When you can deal with everything in this nondiscriminating way, your mind will become exceedingly light." Sodo-san's mind was 'exceedingly light' and that was what lightened the minds of those who came upon him in the park, even if for them it was just for a short time on their stroll.

Like many of his poems, his songs express events of importance in his life. The death of his brother off Midway Island during the Second World War stands out because it was first a poem and then extended to a song. The year was 1942.

Mother
Dear mother
From now on
consider Neptune's sea
to be
your child.

Many of Sodo-san's poems and songs were of daily happenings in his life, usually on a lighter note than the death of a family member. In 1950 while living at Antaiji, in Kyoto, he was introduced to Koumei Shibatani, an elementary school principal and composer of music. They became friends and Shibatani Sensei became his mentor, reviewing his compositions. The first piece Sodo-san showed Shibatani was a song about seeing a newborn praying mantis in the fields of Higo far from his hometown. Shibatani's response after working with Sodo-san composing the melody is interesting:

It matters little who created this piece or who made changes to it. What's important is that the words and the melody exist; that we have this song and melody here now before us and the two of us are working on it. And that this praying mantis was born.

I don't know what Shibatani's relationship to Antaiji was, but that response certainly feels like a Zen response.

The musical performance from this Zen monk sitting in

a bamboo grove in a corner of a park was in itself an attraction. However, I believe it was the joy in Sodo-san's expression, an inviting demeanor, a certain charisma that invited people to approach him. After years of Zen training in temples where he may have felt himself to be the odd man out, he'd finally found a place and a lifestyle that suited him, and his expression was radiant with that awareness.

When we met Sodo-san in the park in 1970, he said he would continue this practice (he considered it religious practice) for twenty years. He was in his thirteenth year at the park at that time. He said making a vow to sit in a park for twenty years was not unusual in the old days. I assumed he was thinking of monks who vowed to live in a forest or under a bridge for a certain amount of time—although his choice was a public park—while sleeping in a boardinghouse seemed to have a bit of a modern touch to it. Selling his compositions on music sheets over which he brushed the words to the songs was still another modern touch. Yet there was something about the way he lived on so little and asked for nothing, and how content he was meditating alone when the winter frost kept people home, that made me feel when I was around him like I was with one of the ancients.

There's a famous legend about a monk who was later called Daito Kokushi (Kokushi being an honorific meaning national teacher) who lived with beggars under the Gojo Bridge in Kyoto. Stories spread of this wise monk disguised as a beggar, and they caught the attention of the emperor, who delighted in conversing with learned monks. Hearing that Daito loved sweet potatoes, the emperor had a plan to search out this learned monk. He brought a basket of sweet potatoes to the beggars and said: "I will give these sweet potatoes to anyone who can step up to them without using his feet." No one moved. Then Daito stepped forward and said, "Give one to me without using your hands." The emperor knew that he had found his man.

Sodo-san spent his time in the park during Japan's most recent affluent period and lived in relatively poor circumstances. Joko's words reverberate in my mind: "My teacher perfected the life of poverty." I'm sure there were many people living on less than Sodo-san. I never felt that he was making a statement about living in poverty. He was just living as simply as he could, with the hope of teaching through his example what a life devoted to zazen means.

Sodo-san practicing zazen in winter at Kaikoen Park

16

A Blend of Zen and Pure Land Buddhism

A monk throws away his home and family, throws away worldly attachments, throws away his body, and throws away his mind. Hence becoming nature as it is.... The only important undertaking for a monk is to uphold and support zazen.

—Sodo Yokoyama

The Universe is practicing zazen. Because everyone practices zazen, I too am able to sit.... Whether you believe it or not, zazen purifies the world.... It's nothing like desire—I practice zazen from a very different place. I am led around by zazen.

—Kosho Uchiyama

All of Buddhism is a footnote to zazen.... Zazen is the way we tune into the whole universe.

—Kodo Sawaki

It is difficult to read these statements and not think that these Zen men are leaving out a very important aspect of Buddhism—compassion. Not much different from the criticism some people give to Theravada Buddhism, that it is only concerned with the individual's search for enlightenment. One has only to look at some of the renowned teachers of the Theravadan school to know that that is not the case.

In an online interview, Joseph Goldstein quoted a Tibetan teacher as saying, "When we realize the empty nature of phenomena the energy to bring about good for others dawns uncontrived and effortless." I suspect if Sawaki Roshi had been asked about compassion, he would say something like compassion is in zazen, *uncontrived and effortless.*

The influence of *Jodo Shin shu,* The True Pure Land sect of Buddhism, is apparent in Sawaki's teaching, and, through him, on the practice of Uchiyama Roshi and Sodo-san. Before Sawaki ran away from home at fifteen years old he'd been raised in a town called Ishinden, run by the abbot of a Shin Buddhist temple, Sen Shu Ji. Sen Shu Ji was in the center of Ishinden; in fact, the town grew from the ever-increasing number of parishioners of the temple. Though he'd grown up outside the moat separating the true devotees of the temple from the riffraff outside, the influence of the only sect in town pervaded both inner and outer Ishinden. The year before Sawaki ran away, he went to many lectures from monks in charge of branch temples in and around Ishinden.

Sawaki's unique interpretation of zazen is at least partly

derived from the influence of Jodo Shin Buddhism. Shin-ran, the founder of the sect, said that he is a deluded person who is saved because of the vow made by Amida Buddha. Amida Buddha vowed not to enter the Pure Land until all those who invoke his name have entered. It is a reliance on what Shin Buddhists refer to as 'other power.' Thinking one can work hard and become enlightened is what many Shin Buddhists would call the mistake of believing in 'self power.' Sawaki's zazen has the flavor of both self and other power. He is quoted as saying he is the most deluded person in the world, which is why he must do zazen. Zazen keeps him from acting out with his deluded self. For Sawaki, zazen is his equivalent to Amida Buddha's vow.

Uchiyama's quote above, that whether we believe it or not zazen purifies the world, is in the spirit of Amida's vow.

Sodo-san decided to practice zazen after reading Zen Master Dogen's *Zuimonki* ("A Record of Things Heard"). He was in his twenties at the time and already had a transformative experience from watching the sunset over a hill in his hometown. But he had yet to overcome a feeling that he was a poor citizen, unable to hold a responsible job. When he heard Sawaki Roshi lecture at one of the main Soto Zen monasteries in Japan, he knew right away that he wanted to study with this man. Here was a teacher who saw zazen as a blessing not unlike the vow made by Amida Buddha.

Sodo-san's father had died earlier that year, and Sawaki may have served as a father figure. Sawaki's zazen—somewhat resembling the vow of Amida Buddha, whom the Pure Land believers refer to as *Oya-sama,* the blessed parent—was the kind of practice Sodo-san needed to deal with the loss of his own father. Sodo-san, like his younger brother disciple Uchiyama, had refined his understanding of Sawaki's zazen over the years.

Kodo Sawaki referred to zazen (his interpretation of zazen, I should say) as "good-for-nothing zazen." My friend, the Reverend Shohaku Okumura, comments on how this type of zazen was a revelation for him. It was the antidote to his life in the Japanese school system, where he was always told things had to be good for something. Everyone, parents, teachers, and the whole of society (as he put it) told him to study hard, get good grades, go to a good university, and so on. As he continued in this practice, he found, after feeling at times like a failure, that this good-for-nothing zazen was in a deeper sense good for something. It taught him that "meaning isn't an objective truth." He discovered in his practice that ". . . help and meaning appear within us and in response to our activity, a meeting of ourselves and all beings."

Shohaku's world is different from the one Sodo-san lived in. Sodo-san lived through the remnants of a society where one was born into a social class and was expected to act appropriately to one's position in that class. Following your own instincts was not considered an option. Though their lifestyles were in some ways worlds apart, Sodo-san and Rev. Shohaku both felt the pressure to be something the outside society had decided was right for them, without consideration of what they thought they should be. Sawaki

Roshi's emphasis on being who you are and not who people tell you to be appealed to Sodo-san and Rev. Shohaku for the same reason. It gave them license to follow their hearts. Both men also found the poetry of Ryokan, the beloved monk who found meaning in the smallest things, to ring true in their lives.

Kodo Sawaki Roshi

17

It Is Okay to Be an Outsider

I'm back in Ojai. Two months have gone by since I visited Joko at his home in Komoro. This morning I was taken aback when I received an email from him. Joko has finally moved into the modern cyberworld. He doesn't even have a flush toilet.

When Mr. Iwazawa, the publisher of *Kusabue Zenji* (*The Grass Flute Zen Master*), brought his laptop over to show Joko what he'd done so far with translating Sodo-san's compositions into electronic music, it must have given Joko the push to join the twenty-first century. He must have felt that a computer was more important than a flush toilet.

Until now my communications with Joko, when I wasn't in Japan, had been through snail mail, which lived up to its name in our case. It would take me hours to compose a letter and then have my wife read it to make sure my Japanese was understandable and polite enough. Then I'd post it and wait a couple of weeks for an answer. By the time Joko's letter arrived I'd have a new question. Now with my Japanese language function on my computer I can easily find the right ideogram and compose a letter quickly. And Joko's response should follow in a day. It's not the same as talking with him at his home, but much better than the old snail mail way.

There are others who knew Sodo-san, but none as intimately as Joko. Even Sodo-san's nephew, Kanjiro (the son of his older brother), whom I met in Sodo-san's hometown and who made part of his house into a Sodo Yokoyama museum, could tell me very little about his uncle. Sodo-san had left Tome City by the time Kanjiro was old enough to remember anything. So his reflections on his uncle were based on what he'd read from the same sources I'd already seen.

When I'd read the biographical notes for "The Woods Where I Stand" (我が立つそま), which said, "Written by Fumio Hatakeyama," I got excited. Another source, I thought. I wrote Joko and asked about this man. "He was Sodo-san's older sister's son," Joko wrote back. "He died in 2008." Foiled again! I hadn't even known that Sodo-san had a sister. Even in the short Taisho Democracy—when a few strong women like Hanako Muraoka, the poet Akiko Yosano, and Raicho Hiratsuka, the champion of women's liberation, spoke and wrote their minds—most women in traditional families remained in the background. I'm not surprised that Kanjiro didn't mention that Sodo-san had an older sister, but why hadn't I asked if he had any female siblings? It would have led me to his cousin Fumio Hatakeyama, who was alive then.

Sodo-san's teacher Kodo Sawaki boasted of following the old ways, not taking a wife. I believe his audience took it to mean he remained celibate, as I did and still do.

One of Sawaki's chief disciples, Kosho Uchiyama, was married twice before he ordained with Sawaki; both wives died before he met his teacher. Uchiyama remained single while studying under Sawaki, but fell in love (his words) while out begging, and married Keiko after Sawaki died and Uchiyama became abbot of Antaiji Temple. There were hardcore disciples of Sawaki who were strongly critical of Uchiyama's decision to get married.

Nothing in Sodo-san's writing even hints at his ever having been in love (other than with zazen).

I lived with a Japanese family for six months at the latter part of my first year in Japan. I took part in the monthly *sesshins* and the daily sittings at Antaiji. Much of the time between my teaching gigs and the temple zazen I spent thinking about how nice it would be to have a girlfriend. I'd go to coffee shops ostensibly to study Japanese, but with the hope I would meet a woman and form a relationship to complete my "ideal" life in Kyoto. Concerned about my drive to awaken to the Buddha mind and what felt like a contradictory drive to have a girlfriend, I decided to talk to my teacher about it. Uchiyama looked at me and said:

"Arthur, you're not the only one who feels this way. I fell in love many times while living the life of a monk."

Kosho Uchiyama, the late abbot of Antaiji

I realized during my stay in Japan that there was a large cultural gap between my Western feeling of a need to have a woman friend to feel complete and the Japanese place for a female companion in the Japanese male mind. Though Uchiyama explained to me that Japanese men who didn't fall in love were the exception, he was not addressing the cultural difference in the meaning of 'falling in love.' I'm sure that the sexual drive in men regardless of cultural differences is much the same. But the idea of feeling fulfilled because you have a boyfriend or girlfriend is certainly influenced by culture. Now that Hollywood movies are worldwide, the cultural gap regarding romance may be closing. In that respect Uchiyama may have been ahead of his time for a Japanese. And that is why he understood my dilemma.

Many of Uchiyama's ideas about life seemed to me to be very Western. It may have made him feel like an outsider in his own culture. His teacher Kodo Sawaki appealed to outsiders. That was one of his attractions to many of his disciples. A lot of artists, who see the world differently from the people around them, must wonder if it is they who have a problem. Sodo-san, the poet, composer, calligrapher, and grass flute musician, is an example of someone who had to search for a place where his unusual lifestyle would be acceptable. To hear from Sawaki that practicing zazen frees you from the influence of the group must have felt like a breath of fresh air to Sodo-san.

18

Sodo-san's Daily Routine—"It's an Easy Life"

My teacher when I arrived in Japan, the abbot of Antaiji, smoked, seemed nervous when he talked, and planned to retire after ten years serving as abbot. None of that fit my vision of an "enlightened" Zen man. I appreciated the schedule Uchiyama set at Antaiji, the community I practiced with, and the freedom I had to take part or not in all scheduled practices at the temple as I pleased. I was young, idealistic, and had expectations, which were not grounded in reality. As time went on I realized how fortunate I was to find a teacher who allowed me to develop as I saw fit, and yet set a rigorous practice schedule to make meditation a part of my being. As I followed the Antaiji schedule, I became more focused on practice and less on personalities that didn't meet my idealistic standards.

When I heard about Sodo-san, this monk who sat zazen all day in a park and played tunes on a leaf, I'd only been at Antaiji for a couple of months. The flames of my idealistic tendencies were fed new fuel. Then I heard that Sodo-san didn't live in the park as I'd thought, but spent his nights in a boardinghouse nearby, I was disappointed. My hope to find a Ramana Maharshi–type saint who cared little for his personal well-being was slowly shattering. In retrospect, I see that those times of shattered ideals were the most important parts of my practice.

When Steve, Lew, and I met Sodo-san in the park and spent some time with him, I felt my former ideals dropping away as I paid attention to the man sitting before me. He seemed content with his life, a result of his love affair with zazen, and that was all I really wanted for myself.

Now, some forty-five years later, Sodo-san's gone, and I'm older than the wise 'old' man was when I met him in the park that day, and I find myself interested in the details of his life in the boardinghouse—the part of his life that shattered my dream of his being another Maharshi. I email Joko with a series of questions.

He responds: "Roshi lived on the second floor of the boardinghouse in a small one-room six-*tatami* space. I lived on the first floor in a larger two-room space with a kitchen. We sat zazen at five in the morning and then had breakfast. After that I went to work. Roshi returned to his room and I guess he used the time before heading for the park to brush poems and songs on music sheets." (He composed many compositions, but the music he sold with his calligraphy was songs others composed from the poems of the famous literary figure, Toson Shimazaki.)

Joko continues: "When I returned from work, I would prepare dinner. Roshi would join me and after dinner he would instruct me on Buddhism. Those were the most joyful times of my life."

In spring of 2012 I had visited Joko and asked if we could walk from what had been his and Sodo-san's boardinghouse to the park just as his teacher had done for the last twenty-two years of his life. Joko took me to the area that had once been the boardinghouse but had since been sold and torn down. What the owner intended for the property Joko had no idea.

We walked south down an incline with the Japanese Alps in the distance visible to the west. Mount Fuji's peak appeared above the clouds in front of us and Mount Izuma was on our right.

"My teacher could view Mount Izuma from his second-floor room on a clear day," Joko commented.

We passed a field of soybeans where the road began to level and then started to climb. The narrow road emptied into a wider road, which we followed to the left. We passed a small park with an *azuma,* a small pavilion, where Joko said Sodo-san would rest when his legs had gotten weak with age. Then he would continue on to Kaikoen Park.

The walk took us about a half an hour. I pictured Sodo-san in his early seventies making the walk back and forth and realizing the trip home was mostly uphill and far more strenuous than the one to the park. I remembered Joko telling me that when Sodo-san's legs could no longer carry him

Joko receiving instructions in the park from Sodo-san

all the way to the park, he would take a cab. It struck me as strange at first, but when I considered his belief that his life in the park was partly a duty that he couldn't shrink from, I viewed it very differently.

"My teacher sometimes practiced zazen in that *azuma*," Joko said when we passed the pavilion, "so he could catch his breath before continuing on."

When Joko talked to me about zazen, he usually quoted from Kodo Sawaki. I thought it strange that he rarely quoted from Sodo-san. When I asked him why, he said, "Sawaki Roshi talked about Buddhism in a broad sense. My teacher sifted the essence from Sawaki's Buddhism."

That didn't exactly answer my question. Joko wasn't trying to deceive me, it was just that his cultural conditioning was more obvious to someone outside of his culture, namely me. On reflection, I think quoting from his teacher was like quoting from his father or an extension of himself. It is not good form in Japan to praise a family member or brag about oneself. I think Joko found it easier to praise the teaching of Sawaki, a man he only knew through Sawaki's books and Sodo-san's talks. He wanted me to understand the proper kind of zazen, but had some internal resistance (perhaps subconscious) to extolling anything he or his teacher (the extension of himself) said. Since the teachings he wanted to impart came from Sawaki (originally from Zen Master Dogen, but through Sawaki's sieve), he found it easier to use examples from his teacher's teacher. It probably felt less like bragging.

After Joko left for work at seven in the morning, Sodo-san would prepare rice balls wrapped in seaweed to take along with him to the park for lunch. He'd return to his room and work on brushing calligraphy on sheet music for travelers who wanted to purchase them. He had three songs that were for sale, all composed from Toson Shimazaki's poems: "First Love," "Separation," and the one carved in a rock at Kaikoen, "Song of a Traveler's Weary Heart by Chikuma River" (see Chapter 4). The first two sold for a hundred yen each, and the longer one—about the castle that is now the park where Sodo-san set up his Temple Under the Sky—was two hundred yen. Then he'd take his lunch, a package of tea, and his brushed songs in a basket and head out to the park, a thirty-minute walk.

I am often brought back to what Sodo-san said when we met him in the park in 1970. Talking about his life—spending every day in the park with the exception of three days when he showed up at Antaiji for Kodo Sawaki's memorial celebration—he said, "It's an easy life." He didn't get bored like most of us would if we spent each day sitting in a park playing a leaf or sitting in zazen. He didn't get bored because he didn't expect anything. He didn't compare himself to anybody. He just did his thing, day after day, and he loved it. That was apparent in his smile.

"My temple," he said, "is the sun, mountain, and blue sky, and the earth is my campground."

19

Satori Is Being Enlightened
to the Fact That We Are Deluded

Sodo-san's teacher Kodo Sawaki was one of the most revered Zen teachers during his life throughout the first half of the twentieth century in Japan. In America, however, he's gotten mixed reviews. His ideas about the value of zazen have not been questioned, but his statements during the Second World War have.

Like Sodo-san, I am interested in Sawaki's view on zazen, not what he said when Tokyo was being firebombed by American planes.

My friend, the Reverend Shohaku Okumura, in his introduction to *The Teachings of Homeless Kodo*, wrote about his understanding of Sawaki, as well as some confusing feelings he had about the complex personality that was Kodo Sawaki. Shohaku elegantly describes how he wouldn't try to apologize for Sawaki's statements about war, knowing Sawaki grew up at a time when Japanese were brainwashed in certain ways that one born after WWII could never really understand. Shohaku focused on Sawaki's understanding of zazen, which he says changed his life.

To quote Shohaku in answer to a friend in Poland who condemned Sawaki's WWII statements as shameful, "I have no words. Sawaki Roshi isn't dangerous anymore. But we are still dangerous."

I believe Sodo-san revered his teacher because of Sawaki's zazen teaching. I don't know if he had any opinion about Sawaki's other writings because he never mentioned the 'other' Sawaki. Like Shohaku, Sodo-san felt saved by zazen, and it was for that reason he felt indebted to his teacher, and why he wanted to demonstrate in his life the power of the practice.

Kodo Sawaki had an array of disciples from different walks of life. I try to understand what it was about this unusual Zen man that attracted so many people who seemingly needed different medicine for their various afflictions.

Kosho Uchiyama and Sodo Yokoyama are the two I've had enough knowledge of to attempt to draw some conclusions about Sawaki's 'silver bullet.' The two disciples appear to have distinctly different personalities. Sawaki reached them on a level I would say had little to do with personality. He took the complex philosophical statements of the ancient Zen master, Dogen, and distilled them into some very practical teachings. The most striking teaching, to my mind, is that one practices for the sake of practice without any thought of gain, *mushoutoku* ('no-gain') zazen.

That Sawaki's two chief disciples should embrace no-gain

zazen leads me to believe that they both felt pressure to be someone important in the world, and because of some feeling of failure in that task they were lost. Sawaki made them see the value of their feelings of failure. It was their porthole into Buddhism. To add to that, Sawaki's injunction that all of Buddhism is a footnote to zazen gave them a straightforward approach to understand the Buddha Dharma.

Sawaki's approach, though not his alone, has a subtlety that is missed by many meditation teachers. He strikes out the idea that meditation will make you a better person. Improving yourself through meditation is not a bad thing, but if your problem is the stress as a result of needing to achieve, the idea of improving through meditation only throws you back in the same arena you needed to break from. Wanting to be enlightened, too, can dump you in the same high-pressured rat race. Letting go should not be so you can become better. It should be for the sake of letting go.

Sawaki realized this in his own life and Sodo-san recognized this too. At a young age (twenty-two or twenty-three) Sodo-san got a hint from the setting sun that he wasn't in control and that that was okay. When he met Sawaki years later, the no-gain zazen resonated with him and he has never felt betrayed by it.

As mentioned in a previous chapter, Sodo-san found a model to emulate in Taigu Ryokan, the eighteenth-century monk who felt he couldn't take over his father's position as village head and ran away to a monastery. Ryokan was a

Kodo Sawaki Roshi in front center, Sodo Yokoyama on left, two rows behind Sawaki

colorful monk whose love of children and sweet innocence made him a cultural hero in Japan. Sodo-san is not well known outside of Kaikoen Park and Antaiji, though he certainly had the color that endeared him to those who came across him while visiting the park.

There seems to be a difference in Sodo-san's approach to the Buddha Dharma and Ryokan's. I wasn't around when Ryokan was alive, so my thoughts are from reading his poems and the stories (many probably myths) about him. Much of my conclusions about Sodo-san are based on his writing too, but I did meet the man. After he played "Old Folks at Home" for Steve, Lew, and me (a welcoming song for his foreign guests), he went into a long rap about the importance of zazen. He didn't give that rap to most of the people who stopped by his Temple Under the Sky, but he knew we came from Antaiji and were interested in his views on zazen.

Ryokan rarely wrote about zazen (though he practiced it) while Sodo-san wrote about it constantly.

Zazen, Sodo-san said, teaches us that we are all ordinary people or deluded beings. We learn that because while we sit deluded thoughts continue to surface one after the other. Our attempt to drive these deluded thoughts away is also delusion, which we learn from zazen. Being aware through zazen that we are deluded, makes us in reality a Buddha. Satori, he said, is being enlightened to the fact that we are deluded. These are teachings Sodo-san learned from his teacher.

"All our troubles in the world, political, economic, and so forth," Sawaki once wrote, "are created from situations in which the awareness of one's ordinariness is absent."

I don't know much about Ryokan's teacher, but I suspect he taught more from the standard Buddhist themes.

Sodo-san's teacher translated Buddhism into ordinary language for ordinary people. Sodo-san understood this and approached his own teaching in a way that would translate clearly to the ordinary mind of ordinary folk. His writing was not that simple, but he taught more through his person—a street entertainer who skillfully slipped zazen into his repertoire.

20

Wherever You Are Is the Best Place to Be

I feel I understand why Sodo-san chose the life he did. Why he chose to move to Komoro and not his hometown, and not to a temple.

In a memoir, the novelist Richard Russo tried to explain why he loved his hometown, Gloversville, but never wanted to return. He found it a lot safer to return to it in the fictitious towns he wrote about in his novels than the powerful reality of returning to the actual hometown.

James Wright, a wonderful poet, left his hometown, Martins Ferry, Ohio, at age nineteen and never returned. Many of his most beautiful poems were about Martins Ferry. He had family there who loved him and who were still living there when Wright died thirty-three years after leaving the town. I wonder whether the poet would have been able to say what prevented him from returning, and if he could, would it have been the whole truth?

Sodo-san's case is a bit different from Russo's and Wright's. He loved his teacher, Kodo Sawaki, who in his eyes was responsible for his introduction to the world of zazen. So he couldn't very well stay away from the memorial ceremonies at Antaiji for the man whose teaching changed his life. But for Sodo-san, the real visits to Antaiji and to his hometown, Tome, were in the many poems and songs he composed about them. And he visited his late teacher, Sawaki, constantly during his daily zazen.

Like so many people who have transcendental experiences in their youth, Sodo-san felt like a loner. From his writing I gather that his father was his first teacher. When his father died, he was lost. Then Kodo Sawaki came into his life. Sawaki taught him the one practice that he could take with him wherever he went and never again be alone. He lived so completely in his music and his zazen that though people admired him, he was not easily reachable on a personal level. His 'castle' in the bamboo grove in a corner of the park was a world that in the modern vernacular might be thought of as a parallel universe. Those who sensed this watched him from a distance; those who didn't entered his castle unawares and left in the same way.

Even Joko, whom I consider a friend and a porthole into the Buddhist part of Sodo-san, did not really know the whole person he considered *his* savior. He recognized his teacher as an artist as well as a teacher of zazen, but didn't seem to have the desire to penetrate the artistic part. If I'd asked him whether he thought Sodo-san lived in a separate universe, I think he would have recommended I get my head examined.

On the other hand, a man who visited the park, and watched Sodo-san as he played the leaf, and who composed this *haiku:*

> *Floating cloud monk*
> *Plays leaf whistle soulfully*
> *Chikuma River*

understood the Grass Flute Zen man. The word for "soulfully" (*kanashii*) in the poem also could be translated as "sadly." I chose "soulfully" to give the poem the depth I believed it had, but "sadly" is also meaningful. This traveler saw, beyond the smiling face of this monk, a world of pathos that the smile guarded carefully. An impenetrable world where the monk lived by himself. The music that he played soulfully gave the traveler a hint of that world, but not a free pass to enter.

So we have a portrait of a man who walked a tightrope between two worlds, as I believe all artists must. Not that people don't appreciate their art, but the soul of its creator is rarely understood. So many artists seek the community of other artists for that reason. Others like the novelist Haruki Murakami and Sodo-san seem to prefer to keep to the world of their own imagination.

"Please, take off your shoes and sit down," Sodo-san told Kyuji Inoue, who visited him in the park as part of an assignment from Daihorin, the Buddhist publishing company. "This is my dragon castle, and I'm Urashima Taro." Sodo-san didn't hide the fact that he lived in a fantasy world where one never ages and life is beautiful. "All you have to do is decide that wherever you are is the best place there is," he continued. "Once you start comparing one place to another, there's no end to it."

Sodo-san was communicative, playing songs on request and selling his calligraphy on music sheets. The songs he brushed and sold were of poems by Toson Shimazaki. He often played those songs on the leaf. But his own personal creations—his *waka* poems that he brushed, especially the ones that revealed the private life of his past—he saved for friends like Kosho Uchiyama.

When the abbot of Antaiji visited Sodo-san at the park, he gave Uchiyama three *waka*. One told of his sadness at the fact that he loved mountains and rivers more than his family. Another told of his feelings for his dead mother, his regrets that he would never see her again. Knowing the monk he'd spent years together training with at Antaiji, he knew Uchiyama would understand his contradictory feeling of love for one's family while apparently neglecting them for the Dharma.

I don't know how Sodo-san's family felt about his becoming a monk and (at least in a formal way) leaving his family for the house of the Buddha. The care that his two nephews put into creating the beautiful book of his writings, calligraphy, and photographs after his death shows the pride they took in how their uncle turned out. His older brother's son,

Kanjiro, has turned half of his home into a museum for the works of his uncle.

Like the loafer, Walt Whitman, the young Sodo-san, who lived in his private world for many years, turned out to be a unique monk who spread the teaching of the Buddha in ways quite unique. Unique even for Zen, which is unique by definition.

Sodo-san doing walking meditation near Antaiji Temple

21

He Sat Expecting Nothing and Yet the Fragrance Spread to Places He Would Never Know

The expression "expedient means" (*houben*, ほうべん in Japanese) was something I always resisted. It seemed to give spiritual teachers a license to do outrageous things under the guise of expedience. Sodo-san's leaf-playing drew people to him and perhaps encouraged some to practice zazen, which he considered his mission while sitting in the park. If he did think of his leaf music as a draw to get people to do zazen, he never said as much. He loved playing music, creating it and brushing it along with his poems, and that's all I can surmise from his writing. He loved being outdoors and entertaining people. Selling calligraphy he'd brushed from the poet Toson's songs seems to have arisen from a need to make some kind of living to pay the rent for his room at the boardinghouse—which makes it an expedient in the secular sense of the word, but not what one would call *houben,* in the Buddhist sense.

Spreading zazen, on the other hand, was something he

considered his duty as a monk and as a lover of the practice. He felt he was not capable of taking charge over monks, so he chose to live the latter part of his life in as natural a way as he could. He believed, as he brushed his thank-you calligraphy to those who gave him a donation after he played a tune for them, that the fragrant mist of zazen would spread a thousand *ri*, a faith in the practice that he carried to his dying days.

Zen is considered the religion of the samurai. Like the warriors who sponsored it over the years, Zen has a reputation for its severity of practice. The Pure Land sects—whose entrance into the Way of the Buddha is through faith—express a gentle side of Buddhism. The simplistic way to compare these two religious sects, even by many scholars, is by calling Zen the "self power" sect and Pure Land the "other power" sect. Another way of looking at these two religious tendencies is as a feminine and masculine side, or as the Taoists describe it, yin and yang. The Taoists see these sides as working together in both men and women, which I believe is a more realistic way of looking at it.

Sodo-san, like Ryokan, appears to have a more prominent feminine side than most Zen monks. His strong expression of faith in the practice he wrote about shows his tendency to be in touch with his feminine nature. One can see it in his delicate calligraphy as well.

Though Sodo-san loved Kodo Sawaki and described zazen in ways he believed were echoing Kodo Sawaki's zazen, he has brought something to the practice that came from him, maybe even from his DNA. And, I believe, Sawaki recognized that uniqueness in his disciple and fortunately didn't try to rid him of it. I don't think Sodo-san felt that kind of acceptance in the temples where he studied; not even at Antaiji, the temple for which he had such fond memories.

It is interesting to realize that Kodo Sawaki had many disciples who might have had difficulty being in the same room with each other for too long. Once Sodo-san went on his own, beginning his truly unique life, he and Uchiyama appeared to get along, and I believe they did. But when they lived together at Antaiji, even the glue that was their teacher Kodo Sawaki couldn't keep them together under the same roof.

Sodo-san had a very powerful experience that I referred to of watching the sunset over the mountain in his hometown. He was in his early twenties at the time. The rest of his life, at least until he found his home under the sky in Kaikoen Park, was the struggle to understand that experience. It was a struggle to understand who he was and to accept himself as that person. As he more deeply understood himself with the help of zazen, the comfort he felt within himself resonated with those who came in contact with him. He expressed it as the profound realization that he was a deluded person. He'd heard Sawaki express the realization of his own deluded nature when Sodo-san first heard him lecture at Sojiji in the late 1930s. Feeling desperate, having lost his father, his first true teacher, Sodo-san went to a meeting at this major Zen monastery outside of Tokyo. Hearing Sawaki's pronouncement of his ordinariness was for him a great relief, but it took many years for it to sink into his person.

The question for many is what does a man spending his days sitting in a corner of a public park meditating or playing tunes on a leaf contribute to waking people up and making our world a better place? Another way of asking that question is, where is the merit in this kind of life? The answer Bodhidharma is supposed to have given when the Chinese Emperor Wu told of all the good works he'd done and wanted to know what merit he had gained was, "No merit at all."

I will answer my question for Sodo-san. "It contributes nothing at all." And yet that is not completely true. Because this man sat in the park maintaining a certain posture and expecting nothing, there was a fragrance that spread a thousand *ri,* a thousand *ri* meaning 'everywhere.' Though not everyone can detect it.

According to Joko, as Sodo-san neared the end of his life he found it difficult to walk to the park, so he would take a cab. The modern-day yogi taking a cab to work. . . . He knew on some level that the power of his 'no merit' zazen would spread the fragrance to places he'd never see. He breathed it and loved it. And as he was dying, it gave him the faith, which allowed him to truly die in peace.

Three days before his death, Sodo-san said, "I am grateful to have been able to study Buddhism, I am grateful to have been able to obtain great peace. I was saved by the sunset.

Sodo-san practicing zazen in a gazebo in the park

The sunset
unaware of the sunset
is still the sunset.

"If people come to visit me," he said on his deathbed, "tell them I said 'thank you.'"

22

Sodo-san in His Own Words

No picture of Sodo-san would be complete without his writings on zazen. And no description of his zazen would be complete without his description of his teacher's zazen.

I remember a talk by Uchiyama, Sodo-san's brother disciple, in which he said that after studying with Sawaki Roshi for twenty-five years he no longer knew which words were his and which were his teacher's. Sodo-san's writings on zazen were mostly in the form of footnotes to his quotes from Sawaki's lectures.

Most of the translations of Sodo-san's writing on zazen here, based on his notes from Sawaki's lectures, come from a book edited by Joko Shibata and published in April 2008. The title *fukan zasou mihotoke* (普勧坐相にほとけ) translated as "The Universal Form of the Buddha." Joko has taken what he considers the important sections from a previously published book of Sodo-san's writing that I have often referred to throughout, titled *waga tatsu soma* (我立つそま), translated as "The Woods Where I Stand."

In what follows below, quotes in italics are from Kodo Sawaki.

The comments are Sodo-san's.

Practice zazen tenaciously and you are Buddha. Sawaki is always a deluded person. However, zazen seeps into Sawaki's blood drop by drop, making him a Buddha, how joyful!

Roshi refers to himself (his individual self) as Sawaki. According to Sawaki Roshi, zazen is not one iota useful to the individual. We do zazen for the sake of zazen. What we refer to as "for the sake of zazen" is its use of this body and nothing else. That is to say we offer this body up to zazen. As described in Dogen's "Rules for Zazen" we stretch our torso, pull in our jaw, place our vision in front of us, and resolve to practice without the least thought of being taken care of by zazen. That kind of resolution is 'no gain, no satori.' It is what Dogen refers to as "Practicing the Buddha Way for the Buddha Way."

Zazen is equivalent to eternal enlightenment of the Buddha.
You need nothing to do zazen—no pen, no notebook. No satori and no delusion is necessary. You need bring nothing with you. It's so vast, so limitless that human beings can't understand it.

[Roshi is talking about] the non-thinking form of seated meditation (no-concept, no-opinion). Nothing is as vast and limitless as non-thinking seated meditation. All the sutras [point to] satori. The *Shobogenzo* [Dogen's "Record of Things Heard"] too [points to] satori. But the non-thinking form of seated meditation goes beyond satori.

Just as we can't calculate the highest common multiple in mathematics, the non-thinking form of seated meditation is beyond [comprehension of] the sutras and the *Shobogenzo*. That's why Roshi said, "Zazen advances even beyond the highest satori."

People want to have a satori like they want a garden in a box. That is not Buddhism.

Don't ever lose sight of impermanence. If you [truly] see impermanence, you are a Buddha with each exhale and a Buddha with each inhale. [You have] everything then and there. No reason to think about persevering in the future.

Zazen is not a competitive Way. You become yourself totally. Zazen is nothing more than becoming yourself.

Though the words "nothing more than becoming yourself" somehow carry with them a selfish sound, all phenomenon, each and every thing, is really nothing more than yourself. A dandelion, which is [an aspect] of all things, is itself completely a dandelion, and doesn't become anything else. It is devoted to itself and nothing else. That is the way of all things.

You never feel that you can catch hold of zazen. You never chase after it and you never run from it. And it is nothing to fear.

This means that you approach everything as non-conceptual, non-opinioned.

No-gain (無所得 or mushoutoku) is the most beautiful aspect of human beings. The aspiration of the Buddhas and patri-archs is to throw away the aspirations of ordinary people.

Try practicing zazen believing you are Buddha and [you are practicing] Buddha's activity. Zazen will naturally become shikantaza. Shikantaza equals Dharma. Zazen is 'playing Buddha'—The Buddha practices Buddha activity. That's what shikantaza is.

It would be great if people came here to practice zazen, unfor-tunately they come because they like me.

It would be great if people came because they liked zazen, but Roshi said they come to his place because of him and there's not much he can do about it. It is nothing more than a result of karma. Zazen is the Way beyond karma. Zazen has nothing to do with accomplished–unsuccessful, like–dislike, philosophy, astronomy, art, etc. All of that is human creation, a result of karma. So it's natural that [zazen], in the light of that, has no benefit. Zazen is useful for zazen only. Roshi wants everyone to practice this kind of zazen, not to practice because they think he is special. Roshi truly [follows] the Way beyond cause and effect. He wants people to understand the meaning: "Zazen equals Buddhahood," "Zazen equals Buddha Dharma."

In whatever you do, if you do it with your whole self you will be "that thing as it is."

This is what is meant by 'no reliance on karma' written in Dogen's "Zazen Shin" (The Needle Point of Zazen). . . . If we don't think in terms of time and space, Buddhahood is always, eternally now. The eternal 'now' is the practice of the *Shobogenzo*. That's why Sawaki Roshi says: "If you can believe in the now, anyone can enter in that moment."

By "entering in that moment" Roshi means "becoming a Buddha."

The Buddha Way is the practice of zazen.

To practice zazen means to make an offer of zazen. It is the expression of zazen, therefore the Buddha Path—This moment directly expresses the Tathagata (literally one who has gone thus)—the Tathagata-Ground which is the Tathagata-Nature, the Tathagata-Countenance and the Tathagata-Body.

"Manifesting the aspects of Buddha-nature is the expression of the bodies of all Buddhas"—This is the meaning of praise for zazen.

In the above "manifest" and "express" mean appear. It is the *genjo* [sometimes translated as life—editor's comment] in Dogen's Genjokoan.

To practice zazen is to die.

These words of Roshi's mean that zazen is the death of the ego, so one is in harmony with the universe—one lives eternally with the universe. Zazen is the path in which we live eternally with the universe. To live eternally with the universe is the way of the parents [the ancestors].

Zazen is becoming a Buddha while you are a deluded person.

In other words you can't say someone who renounces the world (becomes a monk) is without delusions. One is ordained a monk while in possession of delusions.

Zazen is not the way of the world, it is the way of the Buddhas and patriarchs. Which means zazen is renouncing the world.

Just as practicing zazen is renouncing the world, just as one renounces the world while possessing delusions, zazen is practiced while possessing delusions. [Actually] zazen doesn't distinguish between monks and laypeople. If you are practicing zazen you are a renunciate.

A true renunciate should give careful attention to shikantaza (just sitting).

Hence anyone who practices zazen is a true renunciate. [Roshi says] "One should follow [the teaching] of the *Fukanzazengi* (The Universal Rules for Zazen) spreading this universal practice of zazen."

Even though people ordain, [give up their worldly lives], delusions don't disappear. However, when one does zazen, while delusions are there, the zazen posture is the posture of the Buddha. Hence zazen is the Buddha leaving delusions as they are.

Such is the form of zazen, i.e., the zazen posture, the Buddha? The zazen posture isn't aware of the zazen posture, still it is zazen.

*This is Sodo-san's unique expression of realization—that like his expression of the sunset being unaware of it being the sunset yet it is the sunset, so it is with zazen. —Editor.

This is an example of beyond thinking, therefore beyond thinking is Buddha. Zazen according to my teacher [Sawaki] can be done by anyone, and whoever is practicing it is practicing Buddha meditation.

*Though Sodo-san practiced in a public park—playing the leaf and brushing poems as well as practicing zazen—he seems to me to have been taking Zen Buddhism back to one of its roots. His Temple Under the Sky was as sacred as the mountains the Taoist saints hid away in, but in a modern setting, Japanese style.

Epilogue

It's May 2, 2016 and I'm meeting Joko once again near Kaikoen Park. It's been two years. He sounded excited on the phone and I wondered if there was something new he wanted to share with me. He shows up on his motor scooter, we greet each other, and he suggests we go to the park.

We sit by the monument to Sodo-san, listen once more to his teacher's rendition on the leaf of Toson's poem put to music, and move on.

"I want to show you something," Joko says.

I don't ask what, thinking it might ruin whatever surprise he has for me. I follow him on the path around the park until we come to a small two-story wooden structure that I'd never noticed before. I follow Joko up some rickety steps to the first level. Large photos of Kaikoen Park cover the walls, photos of the park all white in winter, in spring with cherry trees in bloom, and many different sections of the park. I can't believe this is what he wanted me to see.

It isn't.

He leads me up some more rickety stairs to the second floor. Aha! The second floor is an exhibit of Sodo-san's calligraphy and photos of him in the park playing the leaf, in zazen, talking with children, smiling serving tea, and much more. Photos I've seen before. There are two CD players on a table in the middle of the room, one with tapes of tunes played on the leaf and sung by the master, and the other with an ensemble group singing his compositions.

"You arranged this?" I ask, feeling it is out of character for Joko to arrange such a show. He is so shy, and it would require some PR work that I can't imagine him doing.

"No," he says with a smile. "The president of the grass leaf–playing group put the show together."

A group of people, encouraged as a result of Sodo-san's legacy (though many of them may not have met the man), meet by his monument every Sunday and play the leaf together.

"I'm getting up there in age and I don't want the teachings of my master to disappear," Joko confesses when we are having tea after arriving at his home and placing incense at the altar in the meditation room where photos of his teacher and Kodo Sawaki sit.

He is seventy-four, the same age his teacher Sodo-san was in his last year. I know he is hoping I will help let Americans learn of his teacher's unique life and message.

We have a simple dinner and spend the evening talking about Buddhism and zazen. He recommends some of Kodo Sawaki's books to me. We also talk about health, and what to do to take care of our aging bodies—an inevitable conversation between two old friends in their seventies.

We sit zazen the following morning. Before I leave, Joko takes me into his bedroom, which is like a shrine room full of photos and calligraphy of writings by his teacher. He shows me a scroll of writing in Sodo-san's flowing script, which I find almost impossible to read. I have to catch a train so we don't have time to talk about its content.

"These reflections are essential to understanding my master's message," he says.

I ask him if he can email me a photo of the scroll and the words written out in a script I can read. He says he will and sends me off with a bunch of goodies for my train ride home—cans of organic juices and bags of snacks, specialties of Komoro.

•   •   •

I am on the train to Niigata. A week has gone by since visiting Joko, and I want to see this part of Japan—the snow country where Taigu Ryokan, the poet-monk who had a great influence on Sodo-san, was born and spent most of his life. Ever since John Stevens published *One Robe One Bowl,* I have had a special feeling for Ryokan's poetry. I also want to see the statue of Ryokan with his begging bowl—which I used in this book. It is a beautiful portrait that seems to express the essence of Ryokan's poetry in this image of the frail, compassionate hermit of Kugami Mountain.

I look for Ryusenji Temple, which houses the Ryokan

statue and the master's grave. I get off the train at Ojimaya Station, walk in the direction I was told, and turn in too early, ending up in someone's backyard. A woman working in her garden asks if she can help me.

"I'm looking for a statue of Ryokan," I tell her.

"That's in the yard of the temple next door," she says. "I'll take you there."

As we walk I ask her about Ryokan. She tells me her name is Kimura, and it was her house where her ancestor cared for Ryokan and where he died. I'd read about Ryokan spending the last five years of his life with a patron named Motoue-mon Kimura, but never expected to meet one of his descendants. Mrs. Kimura is shy and when I ask if I can take her picture she smiles but refuses.

The statue of Ryokan is smaller than I imagined from the photo, but no less powerful an image than I felt from the photo. I thank Mrs. Kimura and return with her to the yard at the back of her home.

"This is the place where Ryokan died," she says, pointing to a patch of land in her backyard. The hut they had built for the aging Ryokan was probably taken down a long time ago.

My next stop is Kugami Mountain where Ryokan's hut, Gogo-an, was. The hut was a replica of the hermit's house, not very interesting, but the mountain where it stood is breathtakingly beautiful. Ryokan's poetry abounds in references to his life on this mountain and the beauty that surrounded him. Despite the long, cold, snowbound winters,

I can still imagine how difficult it must have been for the nature-loving poet to leave such spectacular beauty after twenty-six years when his failing health made living on a mountain impossible.

•   •   •

I am back in California. I open my computer and there is an email from Joko with a photo of the calligraphy and Joko's transcription from the scroll he deemed essential to fully understand his teacher. It is uncannily coincidental that the scroll is full of Sodo-san's praise of Ryokan. The calligraphy and my translation follow.

六月六日は良寛さまのおなくなり
良寛さまのおつかたみでしあり

奴夏此芯に取り残されし窓の月
に任せらる良寛禅師に帰命した
つゝにな気

かたみとて何う残さん春は花
夏ほとゝぎす秋はし立ぢは
あでみの花ハ良寛さまのかたみ
にし玉れば

てよりつき荘びしひとのかたみ
よし今年もまたみ花さきてよし

草地一所又住の旅にして
能く春じことにあさみ花さく

天城山咲き入ませみ美しく
花のさきませめのく春じことに

耕雲相逸

Mother nature is Ryokan-san, and she is Ryokan's keepsake.
She is the moon the thief left at Ryokan's window.
I take refuge in this song through which Ryokan-san [still]
    lives.

  What shall I leave as a keepsake?
  cherry blossoms in spring
  the warbler's song in summer
  crimson leaves of maple in autumn.

Ryokan also bestowed thistle flowers as a keepsake
And playing bounce-ball with children
Thistles bloom this year, a remembrance of his homeless
    travels
    with grass for a pillow

Thistles bloom each passing spring.
Amagi thistle of Amagi Mountain, beautiful flowers in the
    fading spring.

Acknowledgements for
The Grass Flute Zen Master

My gratitude for the assistance by Joko Shibata is apparent throughout the book, as is my amazement at how devoted he is to the memory of his teacher Sodo Yokoyama. Needless to say the book would never have been written without his willingness to respond to my countless enquiries. And for hosting me whenever I went to Japan.

Thanks to Sara Cloud, who suggested I turn my blog into a book, instilling the confidence in me needed to complete the project.

Thanks to Neil Nelson, my poet-confidant, who taught me his 'slash and burn' method when he looked over my translations of Yokoyama's poems—a method truly essential when you are translating *haiku* and *waka*.

Thanks to Ryo Iwasawa for providing me with photos so important to the project.

Thanks to Richard Collins for reading the ms. and making great suggestions. Your support has been very important to me.

Thanks to Juan Medrano for helping me navigate my way through my computer. You take me out of my daydreams and into the 21st century.

Thanks to Jack Shoemaker for recognizing the value in the teachings of Sodo Yokoyama. Jack is a dying breed of editor/ publisher (one who values books and their writers above all). And to the Counterpoint staff who reflected Jacks care for writers throughout the process of publishing the book.

And my eternal gratitude is always to Hiroko. She answered all my questions about difficult passages in the Japanese language, which Yokoyama often created to express feelings that the standard Japanese just didn't cut. And thanks for helping me in other ways too numerous to mention.

Printed in the United States
by Baker & Taylor Publisher Services